This book is dedic
You will never ⌐

DISCLAIMER

After reading the draft of this book my family and friends suggested that I put some kind of disclaimer or something in here, explaining that nothing in this book should be taken seriously and that it's all fiction, or something along those lines. So here it is...

All of the characters and events in this book, even those that might be loosely based on real people, places and scenarios are entirely fictional, any likenesses or similarities to actual people are purely coincidental. Also, this book in no way condones acts of violence, drugs use or any other type of illegal or illicit activity. Don't try this at home...? Don't be a Bastard Teacher!

Hopefully, that's enough to protect me from being sued, sacked or blacklisted from teaching in the future... If not fuck it, I tried.

INTRODUCTION

"After the five years I have spent here I'm glad it's over, the only thing I've enjoyed is seeing my friends every day"

This was my comment in my senior school yearbook but even though I utterly hated school and the bastard teachers that I had, I have been teaching for many years and I love my job.

Teaching truly is an amazing profession to work in, it can be very difficult for many reasons but I have met and helped to shape the lives of some amazing young people and I have met some amazing staff, but as with any job I have also come across some fucking cunts. Yes, some kids are total cunts as are some of their parents and of course some staff. Now you might think that I'm being a bit harsh here especially if you are a parent of a school pupil, you probably think that your child's teachers would never say that about you or your child, but trust me you're wrong. Teachers are just people, and they have normal human emotions, and if you or your kids are pricks, believe me, that's the first thing said about you or them when the staffroom door closes.

Now, again I must stress that there are a lot of lovely students out there, they are friendly, polite and cause no real bother and you may hear about one or two of them in this book. Some have genuine social, emotional, and mental health issues that contribute massively to the way that they behave, but my favourites are the little bastards who just fuck about and make your life hell simply because they enjoy it. Maybe because I was a bit of a bastard at school myself, I see a little bit of myself in them. I don't know but whatever the reasoning I think it's karmically fitting that I am now the bastard teacher because it certainly takes one to teach one.

I have included a few stories from my time as a Newly Qualified Teacher (NQT), working for an agency as a cover teacher and as a teaching assistant at various primary schools, secondary schools, Special Educational Needs (SEN) schools and Pupil Referral Units (PRUs) in England. The majority of these stories are from my time working at a pupil referral unit or PRU, so for those who don't know, I'll give a brief overview of what a PRU is.

A PRU is a school for students who have been deemed too unruly for mainstream schools. They have been permanently excluded from mainstream schools and academies and sent to the PRU where we would be expected to either, help adjust their behaviour and get them back into another mainstream school, assess their needs and find another more suitable provision for them such as an SEN school, or find some other suitable provision for their educational needs. The reality, however, is that many kids get sent to the PRU and are forgotten about by the system.

In the PRU that I refer to in a vast majority of these stories, the classes were generally no more than six students per group. Now if you're a teacher reading this book thinking, six students, is that all? Sounds like a breeze. Then go fuck yourself, imagine the six hardest to teach students you've encountered and imagine trying to teach them all at the same time in the same class. It's not that easy believe me.

Throughout this book you may notice staff seem to appear from nowhere, disappear without mention or a subject teacher switches from one story to another. This is due to the constant turnover of staff. It takes a certain type of person to work in a PRU, it's not for everybody. I have seen so many excellent teachers come and go simply because the PRU environment is not for them, and even those that do enjoy it to begin with can quickly burn out if they are not properly prepared for what they are getting themselves into. I apologise if it's jarring at all but as the great Tupac Shakur once said, 'hey, that's just the way it is.' I will however, briefly tell you a little bit about the headteachers that feature before we get started.

When I first started at the PRU the headteacher was a woman named Sandy. Sandy had great relationships with the students and the staff, was committed to making the PRU the best that it could be and under her management the PRU's Ofsted rating went from 'Requires Improvement' to 'Good'. Sandy opted for an early retirement however when she found out the

PRU was going to be merged with an alternative provision.

Sandy was replaced by a woman on secondment named Liz and she did not make a very good first impression. I know you shouldn't judge a book by its cover but it's hard not to when the new head of the school walks in looking more like brothel madam than a headteacher. Liz was, and I can rather confidently say will be the worst headteacher I have ever worked for. You'll find out why as you read on but for now I'll just say, when there's an arsehole in charge, expect nothing but shit.

After Liz decimated the school budget, took our Ofsted rating from 'Good' to 'Inadequate' and destroyed the staffs' morale, a new headteacher started... and finished on the same day. He came in on the first inset day of a new academic year, gave us all a load of spiel about how he was going to fix everything, take no nonsense from the students and all sorts of other shit and then that was it, we never saw or heard from him again.

About a month later Carter was brought in temporarily. Carter was an old rich guy who was put in place simply to fill the seat and sign paperwork for the merger, interview and employ a new permanent headteacher and make sure that nobody spent a fucking penny.

Carter left after employing a new headteacher, Christine, and an assistant headteacher called Roger who were actually a breath of much needed fresh air.

Now that all of that is out of the way, let's get into the stories.

CHUCKY AND THE CABBAGE PATCH KID

The agency sent me to a primary PRU (yes, they have those), I arrived at reception and introduced myself.

"Hi I'm Marvin Foe, I was sent from the agency."

"Oh yes hi, you're a little early but have a seat, I'm not sure if they want to wait for the others to arrive but I'll check," said the receptionist.

"Others?" I enquired.

"Yes from the agency, there should be few today as we've got a lot of staff off at the moment. Have a seat and I'll get somebody to come down and see you."

A few minutes later the headteacher arrived, he explained that there were a few students that were being kept isolated due to incidents throughout the week and therefore agency staff had been brought in to help out.

"One of the students is here already, his name's Archer, so if you want to follow me I'll introduce you and you can work with him today," he said with enthusiasm.

As we walked to the classroom where Archer was sat waiting, the headteacher told me not to worry about getting lots of work out of him but just to try and keep him busy and contained; away from the other pupils. He explained that Archer was a year three boy that had been removed from his regular class because he was being too disruptive, as were a couple of other year threes. Archer was very small and had a mop of brown hair with a fringe that almost covered his eyes. He was a bit scruffy looking but had a little chubby Cabbage Patch Kid face that you just wanted to grab by the cheeks and wiggle.

He was a bit nervous as I was a complete stranger and was to be working with him one to one, so initially he did not say much, however, after speaking to him for about ten minutes he started to relax a bit and chat to me. During our chat, we came to the agreement that we would do whatever I wanted for fifteen minutes, which would be some kind of work and then whatever he wanted for fifteen minutes which would be some kind of play.

Everything was going well and Archer was getting small amounts of work done in between playing the Nintendo Wii, games on the internet, drawing and having a who can do the loudest burp competition. For one of Archer's fifteen minutes, he said he wanted to look for something to play with in the P.E. cupboard, so we walked down to the hall and I unlocked the door to the P.E. equipment. Archer was in the cupboard and I was stood at the doorway waiting for him to select something to do when I heard a child screaming and heading in my direction. I turned to see a small ginger boy with the grumpiest, scratched up, old man face I have ever seen come hurtling towards me. He looked like the post train track version of the Chucky doll from the fourth Child's Play movie The Bride of Chucky but in a grey Nike tracksuit. He sprinted full speed towards me and at the last second skidded on the gym floor to come to an abrupt halt like the Road Runner, stopping about a foot away from me. The boy cranked his neck right back and looked up staring me dead in the eyes, his pale freckled face was all scrunched up as he scowled at me. I looked around and saw nobody at all, I looked back down at the reincarnated psychotic doll stood in front of me. This is weird I thought to myself, I suppose I should say something to him.

"You alright?" I said using my softest and friendliest tone.

And with that, he sprung into the air, threw his arms and legs out in a kind of flailing star jump, let out an ear-piercing scream, landed and grabbed onto my forearm and bit me as hard as he could. He clamped right down and started thrashing his head side to side like an enraged pit-bull. I was so shocked I turned to the only person I could for help, my new bestie Archer.

"What the hell?" I said in a panic looking at the seven-year-old.

"Get him off! Get him off!" Yelled Archer.

"I'm trying! I'm trying!" I screamed back.

I didn't know what to do, I tried to shake my arm loose

but the kid was not letting go for shit. Options started racing through my head, maybe Archer will save me? No, there's no way a Cabbage Patch Kid could take on Chucky. Punch him in the face? No, upper-cutting a primary schooler will definitely be bad news for my DBS certificate. Scream for help like a little bitch? No, I don't wanna be that guy. Fortunately, someone heard the commotion and came running around the corner.

"Is this yours?" I asked, pointing at the little ginger bastard cannibalising my arm.

"Yes, sorry. I didn't know where he went. I've not been to this school before," he blurted out as he grabbed the boy and yanked him from my arm.

"Oh, are you from the agency?"

"Yeah, I'm with him one to one all day."

After being released Chucky darted off again and the guy chased after him once more. I turned and looked at Archer who was stood silently and perfectly still with a football in one hand and some plastic cones in the other.

"Thank God we were both early to school today hey Archer?"

THE WORST SUPPLY
TEACHER EVER

I think I had been working as a supply teacher for a bit too long and my passion for teaching was starting to falter. Working for the agency doing supply teaching meant that a majority of the time I was teaching a subject that I had little interest in, and going from one school to another every day meant I didn't build up any friendships at work or get to know any of the students very well. As a result, I just didn't really care about doing a good job, I was literally going to schools just for the money (which was shit I might add). The money I was getting just didn't seem worth the amount of effort I would normally put into a lesson, so I simply stopped putting in as much effort.

Everyday I would walk into a school, look at the work that a teacher had left for the class to complete and then say to the students' something along the lines of, 'your teacher has left instructions for you all to complete questions one to ten in your books, as long as you get to question five and don't get too loud I will leave you alone. Now all of you get your phones and head-phones out, put on some music and get on with it.' Allowing most classes to have their phones on and listen to music would normally be enough to ensure an easy time, the students would at first think it's some kind of joke or a trap but then once they realised I was seriously going to let them listen to music on their phones they were silent. Add in the fact that I only want them to do half of the work they have been set, even better, they'd think I was an angel and be as good as gold.

Inevitably there would always be one little shit (almost always a boy) who took my kindness for weakness and decided to act up a bit too much, get too loud and draw attention to himself. So I would immediately blast asunder this delusion and unleash a swift and strict sanction with no second chances. Normally this involved walking over to him, grabbing all of his stuff off of the table and making him sit either on a desk on his own, somewhere away from his friends or directly opposite me (never to the side, you'll see why in a minute). After this, I would announce to the class that if I have to do the same to anybody else in the room EVERYBODY loses their phone and music privileges. The immediate impact of this was that now the rest of the class would police themselves, nobody wanted to lose their phone and music and certainly, nobody wanted to be the person who lost the entire class theirs... Lovely. I would then set up an episode of Family Guy on my laptop at my desk, put my headphones in, sit back and do fuck all.

WHO'S THE
BITCH NOW?

While working in a high school not far from where I lived I had a student called Leroy and I just could not stand him. He was rude, had no respect for anything or anybody including himself, refused to pay attention in class and most of all, he smelled awful. I mean all of the time he just stunk like hell. This is not an exaggeration, I could literally walk into a room or corridor and with the quickest of sniffs know with absolute certainty, Leroy had been there recently. In fact, it was one of the games we would play as staff. Not only was his stench bad but it was it unique, like an old man who got sprayed by a skunk, died and was beginning to rot away. Honestly, you could track him down like a hound if you wanted to.

So one day I walked into the classroom and written on my board was 'Mr Foe is a bitch and if u wanna now who rit this go ask Leroy!' I knew from his shitty spelling who had 'rit' it but I sniffed him out and asked him anyway.

"Leroy," I said calmly. "Do you know who left an inappropriate message on my board?"

He and his friends began to chuckle.

"Yeah I did it and what?!" He said proudly. "You are a bitch so what you gonna do?"

I thought about putting him in detention, but the thought of having him in my classroom stinking the place up for an hour after school on a Friday, when I could be at home on my sofa watching TV with my family was enough for me to abandon that immediately. So instead I adopted a more nonchalant response.

"Don't do it again," I said nicely and I walked away.

The next day I was walking to the local newsagents and who do I see standing outside of the shop? Leroy and his little cronies.

"Aaaah, Mr Foe... You! Bitch!" He shouted as I walked towards the shop doors.

I turned and looked at him, he was laughing hysterically with his mates. I could feel the rage bubbling up from my torso into my head. I shook my head and told myself to leave him alone and took another step towards the shop, with that step these words left his mouth.

"Little pussy hole bitch."

That was it, I wanted to pummel his face into an unrecognisable amorphous mess of flesh and bone. I slowly paced towards him, leaned in as close as I could without vomiting, stared deep into his soul and whispered what is potentially the worst thing I have ever said to a student during my career.

"Listen up Leroy you little fucking shit stain, we're not in school now, so if you talk to me like that again I'm going to kick the fuck out of you in front of your little dickhead mates. Remember, I'm at your school on supply so if I put you in hospital it doesn't really matter, I'll just go to another school."

What can I say, I'm not perfect, but strangely enough ever since that day he was very polite to me.

THE SILENT
TREATMENT

I used to get bored as a supply teacher and so I would try to come up with ways to keep myself entertained. One of my favourite things to do in mainstream schools went like this. I would walk into the classroom, write my name on the board and the task that the students needed to do. As the students walked in I would nod slightly to them but not say hello and put my index finger to my lips indicating that they should be quiet. Next, I would point at the task and information on the board and then gesture with my hand for them to get on with it. Again I would say nothing.

At this point, because I hadn't said a word the students would start to get slightly freaked out and generally whisper to each other. I would then walk around the classroom very slowly, with a poker face as they got on with the work making intense eye contact with any students who spoke too much. If a pupil got too loud (which in an almost silent room basically meant doing anything other than whispering to the person next to them) I would first write 'Shhhhh' or 'STOP TALKING!' on a post-it note. I'd then walk by them and as I passed their desk I would stick it on their desk in front of them and keep walking. If they got loud again I would quietly and calmly walk over pick up their stuff and move it somewhere else in the room away from everyone else, again saying nothing in the process. If a student asked for help with the work which they wouldn't usually because they were probably borderline terrified, I would point at the information in their books, or write things down on post-it notes and give it to them. Keeping this going for an hour-long lesson was a challenge and the atmosphere in the room sometimes got a little intense, but it was worth it because here came the most awesome part. The lesson ends, the bell rings and I would say, in the happiest, friendliest and most upbeat way possible.

"That was great guys, really good stuff, well done I hope you enjoy your next lesson."

Then wave bye to them with a massive smile as they left confused about what the hell just went on.

I GOT PIMPED OUT

The agency sent me to an SEN school and told me I was going to be a TA, when I got there it turned out I was not going to be a TA at all. Instead, I was with another guy from the agency and we had the pleasure of dealing with one student for the day who had been removed from his group because he could no longer be trusted in there. His name was Gary, he had quite severe autism and spent the entire time saying either 'pinch' while he attempted to pinch us, 'scratch' while attempting to scratch us, or 'touch your winky' as he tried to touch our penises.

We were located in a small house on the school site that had been converted slightly into a sort of sensory/isolation building, and our entire job was basically to keep Gary on the ground floor of the house and try not to get molested. This went on for the entire day, literally nonstop, six and a half hours of rape dodging. Occasionally we'd put him in the garden and watch him through the window so that we could go to the toilet or eat some lunch but other than that, it was relentless.

At the end of the day, Leanne from the agency called me.

"How was your day?" She said all chirpy.

"Well, I certainly wasn't a TA. You're paying me my teacher day rate for that." I replied bluntly.

"They want you back tomorrow, shall I put you down?"

I paused for a moment as I quickly figured out in my head how much money I had earned for the week so far.

"Teacher full day rate?" I asked.

"Yeah."

"And for today?"

"Yeah, no problem."

I paused again as I weighed up the pros and cons of fending off the winky toucher for another day. Yes, he's going to try and sexually assault me for six and a half hours but I've got rent to pay.

"So, tomorrow? Shall I put you down?"

I took a deep breath.

"...Sure."

THE STREAKER

I was sent by the agency to work at an SEN school and was sat in the classroom reading the student profiles. There were only four students in the class but due to their varying levels of need, I had a lot to read through. I had been to this particular school a couple of times before so I sort of knew one or two members of staff there, but the class that I was working with was completely new to me.

Whenever I started with a new class at any school, I would try to find out key bits of information from the permanent staff about the students. They know the children better than anybody else and as much as they might give you a bit of time to go through pupil profiles, (if you ask and if they have them available and updated), there's never enough time to A; go through them all and B; retain all of the information about people you have not even met yet. Just asking the staff was usually enough to get the most vital and recent information about things to be on the lookout for and which students were likely to be the most problematic.

Stuart was the permanent member of staff and there was me and two other agency members of staff in. I asked Stuart.

"So what's this group like? Is there anything or anybody in particular I need to be aware of today?"

"Nah, we should be fine, there's plenty of us in today." Stuart replied confidently. "This group is mostly Asperger's but they're pretty sound. Just try and keep the door shut because Lucy will try and get outside."

Lucy was fourteen with moderate symptoms of autism, she hardly spoke anyway but spoke even less due to being in a room with so many new faces. She sat in her chair very subdued as she slowly and painstakingly decorated her work with glittery gel pens. Now when Stuart said Lucy will try and get outside I assumed he meant she would try to wander out of the classroom, maybe go and hide somewhere, disrupt other classes or go off to find her favourite member of staff. So when partway through the lesson Graham, another guy from the agency, came back from the toilet and left the door to close on its own neither of us expected what happened next.

Lucy got up and she darted through the door like Usain Bolt. Graham and I looked at each other in shock, we had no idea she could move so quickly.

"Go and get her quick!" Yelled Stuart in a panic.

Graham and I went out of the door after her.

"What the fuck mate?" I said to Graham as we ran across the car park.

"I know, I'm sorry man I had no idea," he said.

"Don't worry, let's just get her quick."

As we ran across the car park a minibus was coming in through the gate and Lucy took the opportunity to get off of the school grounds. As we started to make up a bit of ground on Lucy she decided to start shedding clothes and continued to run. When we managed to catch up to her she was completely topless and had no trousers on. We managed to hold her but she was fighting really hard, so trying to get her back to the school was proving unbelievably difficult.

Now picture the scene, two adult men, wrestling an almost naked fourteen-year-old girl in broad daylight in the middle of a residential road... We had to transport her a few hundred metres back to the school but because she was fighting so much and because we were trying to be very careful as to where we placed our hands it took a while. Nonetheless, the police were at the scene extremely quickly, to be honest, I don't know how they managed to get there so quickly because it felt like we'd only been out of the school grounds for a minute or two but either way they arrived and pulled up alongside us.

"What's going on here gents?" Said the first police officer.

"Let go of the girl," ordered the other.

"We know it looks bad guys but she's from that school there, we work there and we're trying to get her back." I said while trying to hold onto Lucy with one hand and show my ID badge that was hanging from my lanyard with the other.

"She's got special needs, it's an SEN school." Graham added.

"Right, let her go then," said the officer again.

"Look, if we let her go she's going to run and then she's your problem. Do you want to help us get her in the car?" I said.

The officers looked at each other and then helped us get her in the car, once she was in the car I gathered her clothes while Graham continued to chat with them. I passed them the clothes and they drove her back to school.

Once we were back in the classroom we told Stuart what had happened and explained to him that she started to strip off her clothes.

"Yeah she did that last week as well, she does it so you won't restrain her." Stuart responded.

"Jesus Christ Stuart. So you know when I asked if there was anything or anybody in particular I need to be aware of today? Do you not think…?"

"Yeah, I should've mentioned that shouldn't I?"

"Yes you fucking should."

BUILDING TRUST
WITH BLU-TACK

It was my first day at the PRU, I was sent there through the agency to cover for the absent Art teacher. Upon arrival, I was greeted by the headteacher, Sandy, who after a quick tour of the tiny and dilapidated building walked me round to the art classroom and introduced me to a teaching assistant named Doris. Doris was an old lady, with a mini afro like Annie from the musical but silvery white. I'd say she was definitely in her mid to late sixties, a little over five feet tall and probably weighed nine stone if her clothes were soaked through. She was very softly spoken and was more than happy to show me where I could find the resources I needed around the room.

"You'll just have two-year eights in the first lesson," she said as she took their books from the cupboard. "They won't do any work but I'll still get the books out just in case, you never know." She smiled and crossed her fingers. "Jim is hard work, very hard work, ADHD, mental health issues, language is a major issue with him, can get aggressive, spitter... Have you worked in a school like this before?"

"Similar." I answered as I locked my bag away. "I'm sure I'll be fine."

Doris continued giving me the rundown.

"Pete is the other one, he'll come in and lie down on that shelf."

She pointed to the shelf underneath the countertop that spanned the length of the room. This is fucking weird I thought to myself, but let's just see how it goes. A couple of minutes later, Pete walked into the room, he was small, slightly chubby and barely made eye contact with me, and just as Doris had said he went straight to the shelf and lay down.

"I'm not doing art I'm going sleep," he said firmly.

I introduced myself to Pete and asked him why he was on the shelf rather than a chair, he told me that he always lies on the shelf and then pointed to the words 'Pete's shelf' that were carved into the edge of it. Can't argue with that level of dedication to laziness, I thought to myself. Pete and I chatted for another couple of minutes as I explained to him that if he did not want to do any work I didn't mind as long as he stayed in the room and didn't cause any problems. He told me about his favourite hobby which was fishing and we talked about Call of Duty. Then Jim walked into the room, Jim was also small but slim, his hair was a brown moppy mess and his clothes were scruffy, his sleeves were rolled up to his elbows and he looked at me as if I had just bitch-slapped his nan.

"Who the fuck's this lanky cunt?"

I liked this kid already, as I was the only person in the room above six feet tall I assumed he was referring to me.

"I'm Mr Foe, I'm covering for Mr Hartford".

"Yeah well the last one they sent lasted a day so we'll see how long you last," he barked.

Jim then produced a large ball of blu-tack from somewhere.

"Where have you got that from Jim?" Doris asked politely.

"None of your fucking business coffin dodger," he snapped clenching the ball in his fist.

Pete laughed hysterically.

"Gimmie some Jim," he said with an outstretched hand.

Jim broke a chunk of blu-tack off and threw it to Pete but I caught it mid-flight. Jim immediately began to get agitated and demanded that I gave it back. Doris told Jim that he needed to hand the rest of the blu-tack over and this enraged him further. I told Jim that he could hang on to the blu-tack and that I would give him the blu-tack that I had back at the end of the lesson if he calmed himself down, I then broke what I had in half and gave a chunk to Pete. I then sat and began making a little man out of the blu-tack whilst telling the boys a story, about a time when I was at university and one of my friends spent over an hour mould-ing an intricate elephant out of blu-tack, and the moment he'd finished, another one of my friends asked to see it and instantly squashed it just because he wanted to see his reaction. They found the story funny and the rest of the lesson flew by.

At the end of the lesson I turned to Jim.

"I'm going to give you this blu-tack back even though I don't think you are supposed to have it, please don't make a mess with it and give to me or Doris at the end of the day," I said.

Jim agreed and I handed it back to him, we bumped fists and he left. As he walked out of the door he turned to Pete.

"He's alright," he said quietly.

Pete nodded. "Yeah he's alright."

GIDDY UP BITCH!

I was asked to go back to the PRU by the agency. This time I was there as a TA and my first lesson was maths. The teacher, Wesley, was stood at the front of the room teaching and I was sat next to a student. Everything was normal until in walked a scrawny, freckled year nine boy with a ginger crew cut, he walked with his shoulders hunched and his arms slightly out to the sides, like he was starting a fight. His eyes were always slightly squinted and his eyebrows scrunched as he scanned left to right suspiciously. His movements were always very sharp and kind of robotic. When he turned he would spin on his axis as if the direction he wished to face had been carefully calculated on a computer and beamed into his brain, he'd then speed walk in a straight line to wherever he wanted to go before halting abruptly.

Upon entering the room, he said nothing. He immediately marched to a chair, stood on it and then climbed onto the desk. With his knees slightly bent and the most serious look in his eyes he began to bounce up and down ever so slightly and rock back and forth. Wesley stood obliviously at the front of the room still writing on the board and the other students did not say a word, they sat in their chairs and continued as normal. I thought for a second, am I the only one who is seeing this? Why is nobody finding this odd? And then it happened, the boy leapt through the air like a possessed squirrel and landed on Wesley's back who yelped in shock.

"Wooohoooo!" Screamed the boy. "Giddy up bitch, giddy up! Yah! Yah! Yah!"

Wesley began thrashing and swinging violently in all directions trying to shake the crazed child from his back, but clearly, this was not the boy's first rodeo. The other students were howling with laughter as I stood up confused, shocked, frozen, I just stared at them as Wesley's arms flailed like one of those blow-up things that you see outside of car dealerships in American TV shows and the tiny ADHD ginger lunatic squealed with excitement.

After what must have been at least fifteen seconds, the boy released his victim and marched out of the door, again he said nothing, just span on his axis and power walked out of the door as I followed behind him.

"Hey, excuse me, hello, yo, oi you, what the hell was that all about?" I said.

The boy just continued walking as if I wasn't even there, I was looking around and there was nobody else about to help me. The deranged cowboy then went straight into the sports hall and picked up a basketball, he stood at the free-throw line and hit three baskets in a row, swish every time like it was nothing.

"You alright?" I said tentatively.

"Yeah, why?" He immediately responded.

"Just asking... What's your name?" I said as I passed him the basketball.

"Jamie Parker," he said before sinking another basket.

"Nice shooting Parker," I remarked.

"Thanks," he replied. "You want a shot?"

SHOW A BIT OF
RESTRAINT

Restraining students is never a nice thing to do and is avoided as much as possible, not only can it be humiliating to the student but it can also permanently damage a positive relationship that you have built up with a student, especially if it was not warranted. The trouble is that when you are working with students in a PRU using restraint techniques is pretty much an inevitability.

Before I was trained to use restraint techniques or 'positive handling strategies' or 'restorative physical interventions' or whatever other friendlier sounding names people have given them, I witnessed my first restraint in a PRU that I was working at for the day through the agency. I went there as a teaching assistant and although I had been to a few PRUs already I had not seen any restraining take place before.

At this PRU the students were kept in the same classroom

with the same staff all day, they never left the classroom for anything (other than to go to the toilet I would imagine). I was asked to go and collect the lunch for my class and bring it back to the classroom, on my way to get it I walked around the corner to see a boy face down on the floor with his face pressed into the carpet, as three members of staff pinned him to the floor. The boy screamed and swore at them with unfiltered hatred and animosity, his face was red all over one side from being rubbed against the carpet, his shoes were removed and tossed to the side and everybody was shouting at once. I remember pausing in shock as I walked through the double doors, I briefly made eye contact with the boy and for that moment I felt awful. The scene resembled someone being arrested by plain-clothed police officers for drunk and disorderly conduct after a weekend bender in the city centre. It might have been easier to look at if the boy was at least a little bigger, but if I had to guess his age I would say he was eleven or twelve.

Seeing a child pinned to the floor by adults is jarring to say the very least, especially when you don't understand why and how the techniques are used. Knowing what I know now about restraints the boy should not have been in any pain whatsoever (oddly being held in a correct restraint position is actually quite comfortable) but when you hear screaming like that it's hard to think otherwise. Having said that, I also now recognise that their communication during the restraint was appalling and probably wasn't making the ordeal any easier for anybody involved. Anyway, after taking a moment to really consider what I was witnessing, I assumed that he did something that warranted the restraint especially as there were multiple members of staff involved and cameras everywhere. Concluding that despite my lack of understanding at the time, what they were doing must have been above board I quickly snapped out of it and continued on my way to get the lunches.

When it comes to using physical restraint, some teachers, although they don't necessarily seem to enjoy it, I feel are very quick to do so and often unnecessarily. I can understand why and how it happens as when a child is not following simple instructions and is instead shouting abuse at you for hours if not days on end, eventually you feel like dragon punching them through the ceiling. It takes the patience of Buddha to work with these types of students and some people just don't have it.

Over the years I have worked with some teachers who in my opinion like to restrain kids, I assume it makes them feel big and tough to manhandle an unruly child but obviously they are just pricks. I remember a guy called Des, who came to the PRU from the agency and stayed for a couple of months was shocked and quite frankly he seemed pretty gutted that there was hardly any restraining going on. He would constantly mention how if a kid spoke to him disrespectfully in his previous school he would 'disable the arm' so that 'they would learn their lesson.' Like I said he was a prick and I assume just taking out his frustration with being short and balding on children who were clearly weak and powerless.

I have completed the Team-Teach and Prime versions of de-escalation and restraint techniques multiple times and unfortunately, I have had to use them several times too. When I first did Team-Teach training it was through the agency, they were sending me to a lot more PRUs because I consistently got good feedback from them, and because I was one of the few who enjoyed working in PRUs far more than boring as fuck mainstream schools. Some PRUs however, would only take agency staff who had this training.

During the training, there are a range of verbal and non-verbal techniques shared to avoid having to put hands on a child which was interesting and very useful. A lot of it is common sense to be honest, but still, it is good to know and obviously needs to be stated for the likes of Des.

The weirdest thing about doing this and other similar training, is when they discuss the law regarding physical interventions and everybody in the room suddenly comes to the realisation that legally you can do anything to a student as long as you can justify it as reasonable, proportionate and necessary to prevent them from harming themselves, others or damaging property. That's right ANYTHING, think about that for a minute, it's crazy. I could kick a kid down a flight of stairs and have no legal consequences. I'm not saying that I have or that I'm going to (although I'm sure I've probably considered it at least once). Seriously though, as long as it was reasonable, proportionate and necessary, and I was able to stand up in court and defend my position it would be fine and perfectly legal.

This law is something that parents and students need to fully understand. Anybody at the school can do anything to a child as long as it is reasonable, proportionate and necessary. Parents of students who have been restrained are often the most annoying part of a restraint, to be honest, there's always the one who comes in and tells you that touching their kid in any way, shape or form is illegal and that they're going to sue you and all sorts of shit. I obviously understand that they are upset but at the same time, I feel like screaming at them to shut the fuck up because they clearly have no idea what they are talking about.

Ok yes, I was being hyperbolic when I mentioned booting a student down the stairs, however, I'll give an example of a scenario whereby hurricane kicking precious little Timmy from the first to the ground floor would not result in a swift change of residence to the local HMP. Let's say this kid was charging up the stairs with a knife, I turn around and he's coming at me full speed screaming 'I'm going to kill you, you fucking cunt!' While swinging the blade in the air, and I have no time or place to turn and run. The spirit of Bruce Lee possesses my body like a poltergeist and I flat foot the shank swinging psychopath straight in the solar plexus sending him headfirst down the stairs. Was it reasonable? Yes, he was trying to kill me. Was it proportionate? Yes, he was trying to fucking kill me. Was it necessary? YES! HE WAS TRYING TO FUCKING KILL ME! Obviously, if little Timmy threw a pencil across the classroom so I quoted Ezekiel 25:17 at him before striking him down with great vengeance and furious anger, that's not going to be as easy to defend in front of a judge.

ADVICE FOR THE
OFSTED INSPECTOR

Ofsted were in the PRU and an inspector came to observe my lesson. I was teaching Jim one to one which was extremely difficult as he never did any work... EVER! Jim was a funny kid, he was a bit crazy and had ADHD so he was very difficult to focus, but he and I got on well.

The Ofsted inspector walked into the classroom, he was about sixty years old, tall with white hair around the sides of his head and bald on top. He wore an expensive-looking and well-fitting grey suit, with brown shoes polished so pristinely that you could see your reflection in them. As he entered the room with his clipboard resting on his left forearm and his Parker pen twirling between his index and middle finger he said nothing. He looked at me and pointed to an empty chair at the back of the room with his fountain pen and sat down. Jim said nothing, just stared at him as he sat down in the corner. I wrote my learning objective up on the board and before I could even get a word out to start the lesson Jim politely asked.

"Sir can I have a pen and paper please?"

Oh my fucking days, I was stunned, I could not believe my ears, he asked for a pen and paper, he even said please. Honestly, I was so shocked that I just whacked them down in front of him as quickly as I could. Jim then turned his back to the Ofsted inspector slightly, covered his paper with his left arm and leant over it while he wrote. I stood looking at him confused, I hadn't asked him to do anything yet, I had literally written the date and a learning objective on the board that was all, but he was writing so I stood and said nothing just waiting to see what he was going to produce. Jim folded the paper in half, then in half again, then without looking in the Ofsted inspector's direction he held his arm out with the folded paper waving it in front of his moody old face. The inspector took the paper and looked at me, I stared blankly back at him as I had no idea what was going on while he unfolded the first fold. I looked at Jim who was sat nice and quietly watching as the second fold was opened up even more slowly than the first, revealing the words FUCK OFF! In huge letters. Jim then launched up out of his seat like a jack in the box and started shouting aggressively at him.

"YEAH! GO ON FUCK OFF! NOBODY WANTS YOU HERE YOU WANKER! FUCK OFF! GO ON! FUCK OFF YOU FUCKING WANKER!"

Jim repeated this with more and more venom every time and the inspector quickly scrunched up the piece of paper and threw it in the bin as he hastily exited the room. I turned and looked at Jim in shock, my eyes wide open unable to blink and my mouth wide open unable to speak.

"What the hell was that?" I eventually managed to utter.

"I done that for you, Sir," he replied. "You don't want some old cunt in here telling you how to do your lessons do ya?"

THE INTERVIEW CANDIDATE'S PRE-DICK-AMENT

Interviews were being held at the PRU and a candidate came in to do her observed lesson as part of the interview process. She was being observed by Sandy and and a woman called Barbara who was the head of the local authority's alternative provisions. There were three students in the class but the candidate had prepared a lesson where the students needed to work in pairs. As one of the students, Chris, did not have a partner Barbara decided to step in and be his partner for the activity. The task was to stand back to back with your partner and describe to them something that they had to then draw based on your description and instructions. Chris began describing to Barbara what she needed to draw.

"Draw a circle at the bottom of the page... Now draw another circle next to it so that the side edges are touching... Now draw a straight line from the middle point of the top edge of the circle on the left that goes halfway up the page and then goes across to the right and then back down to meet the middle point on the top edge of the circle on the right."

Now his description was brilliant, however, most people would at this point realise what they were drawing and put a stop to it, but no, he continued to describe the image to her and she continued to draw a massive cock and bollocks, complete with pubic hair, a relatively detailed bellend, veins and at the point when she was just about to draw sperm shooting out of the top the candidate had to intervene, that's right THE CANDIDATE had to tell Barbara to stop drawing the ejaculating penis and to put the paper down. The students were absolutely pissing themselves laughing, Chris then quickly grabbed the drawing from the table and ran to my classroom to tell me all about it... For some reason the candidate didn't get the job.

HIGH AS A… CAT?

I was being observed by Sandy as a part of my performance managment as an NQT. In the class, there were only supposed to be two year-ten students, Bobby and Gary. Gary was on time and ready so I started the lesson without Bobby. It was a music lesson and I was teaching them to recognise and identify the keys on a piano keyboard. I had a small keyboard with me and had printed out a picture of a keyboard that they needed to label the notes on. I explained to Gary that to identify the keys on a piano he should first of all look at the black notes, there will always be two together and then three together.

"Think of the two black notes together as the walls of a dog kennel and the white note between them is the dog inside the kennel, so this note is D for dog." I said as I held up the keyboard and pointed at the keys. "Now if you know that this white note is D, what do you think this note is?"

I pointed to the white note to the left of D and he responded.

"Is it C?"

He was correct and I was feeling pretty good about things.

"Now if you know where C is and where D is, and you also know that the white notes go from A to G you should be able to label all of the white notes on the keyboard."

Sandy seemed happy so far and I gave Gary a worksheet to see if he could label all of the white keys on his own. At this point, Bobby walked into the lesson and sat down. It was overtly obvious that he was absolutely high as fuck, his blood red eyes were barely open, he had that cheesy little stoner grin and he absolutely stunk of weed. The first thing out of his mouth was.

"Sorry I'm late sir, I had to kidnap some dickhead."

I mean what the fuck do you say to that? I looked at him with confusion and after a brief miniature internal panic attack where I considered addressing his confession to a crime as an excuse for his lateness, whilst simultaneously thinking he's going to fuck up my entire lesson because he's too wasted to understand anything, I just pretended like he never said it. I just completely ignored it and thought to myself well whoever this victim is, they're not jeopardising my chance of getting a grade one rating for this observation, the safeguarding form will have to wait. I put the piece of work in front of him and started to teach him how to identify D on the piano using the exact same method that I used with Gary.

"So these are the two black notes, think of them as a dog kennel..." I began to explain.

After giving him all of the information I then asked him which note I was pressing down. I was holding the keyboard up and pressing the D key, the note I just taught him two seconds ago. Bobby looked at me with his eyes glazed like a Krispy Kreme doughnut and responded in the laziest tone ever.

"Fuck knows..."

I wanted to slap him and scream wake the fuck up you half-baked little shit I'm in the middle of an observation, but I refrained and took a deep breath.

"Remember Bobby, two black notes together, dog kennel, what note is this?"

"Dog?" He replied.

"Well... sort of... it's just D, but yeah D for dog."

I then pointed to the white note to the left of D and said.

"Since all the notes go in alphabetical order, what note do you think this might be?"

There was the longest pause ever. I stood looking at him whilst in my mind screaming the answer at him, C Bobby, the answer is C, c'mon man this is simple shit. Trying to do some Derren Brown style mentalism shit on him. Just say C, C for cunt you little cunt come on. Bobby looked me dead in the eye, ever so slowly pointed his index finger at the keyboard that I was holding in front of his face and said.

"Cat?"

I did not know what to do, was he right? Was he just trying

to think of an animal beginning with C because of the whole D for dog thing? Was it simply word association, I said dog so he said cat? Well, I'll never know, the lesson ended. What I do know however is that a couple of weeks later Bobby's Mom came to parents evening, so I sat her down and spoke to her about her stoner son.

"Your son comes to school and he is so high that I just can't teach him anything."

To which her response was.

"Yeah I know what you mean, I'm at the point now where I can't have him smoke it in the house because it stinks the whole house up, I make him go in the garden."

I sat there for a good few seconds just stunned, my mouth wide open as I looked at this woman seeking sympathy from me. I felt like leaping out of my chair and backhand slapping her on the cheek so hard that her face span round to the back of her head. I mean what kind of response is that? Fortunately, I'm a god damn professional so instead, I just told her it was nice to meet her and that she could leave now.

THE PHOTOSHOP
REVELATION

Laura was a strange character, she was in year ten and had been at the school since year eight. For all intents and purposes she should not have been at the at school, she was never actually permanently excluded from a mainstream school but was instead sent to the PRU 'temporarily' while she awaited a place at a local school after being placed in care, and then basically forgotten about. She was the definition of the word average in every way, which in a school like ours meant she stuck out like a drag queen in a nunnery.

Laura was of average intelligence for her age but again due to the types of students that we generally had at the school, this made her noticeably more intelligent than most of her peers. This was something that she loved and constantly projected, rubbing it in the faces of the other students, which as you might imagine they did not take too kindly to. She would do things such as correct their grammar and pronunciation when they spoke, intentionally look up and use words that she assumed they wouldn't understand and then explain what the word meant as if they were toddlers, once I even saw her mark a student's work as if she was their teacher. In response to this, the student emptied the contents of a bin over her head, then put the actual bin over her whole head and punched it several times as hard as he could. Now I'm not saying that this kid handled the situation perfectly but let's be realistic, she had to expect something bad to happen. I mean did she honestly think he was going to say, 'Thanks Laura, I'm so glad that you drew red crosses all over my maths work and wrote YOU SHOULD KNOW THIS BY NOW, TRY AGAIN!' No, obviously not.

As a member of staff, the issue that you had with Laura being bullied was that you felt bad whenever she was targeted but you understood why it happened. Part of you always thought, she's kind of asking for it really and she does nothing to help herself. Laura would walk around with a pencil case in one hand, which was something that nobody did because the school provided all resources in each lesson, and a stack of textbooks that she was taking home for homework in the other. Homework which she would ask staff for because the very idea of a teacher giving out homework to any of these students and expecting it back was fucking hilarious. Not only that but if anybody ever offered to put her homework in reception for her to collect at the end of the day she would refuse. Why? So that all of the other students would see her walking around with lots of books all of the time, carrying them from lesson to lesson like she was better than them, drawing in the attention she was seeking.

Laura also called all staff by their first names, personally, I didn't really care about that but some staff did and would tell her not to do it, but it was just another thing that she did to try and appear to the other students that she was above them, in my opinion. Laura was offered places at other schools but refused to accept them as she preferred to stay at the PRU. I suppose she recognised that in a mainstream school she would not get as much care and attention from the staff and she would also be middle of the pack in terms of her academic ability and intellect.

One day during a lesson Laura mentioned some celebrity I'd never heard of, so I looked her up on Google.

"She's beautiful isn't she Marvin?" She said.

"Meh, she's not really what I'd go for, to be honest, plus that picture has clearly been heavily photoshopped." I replied.

"She's clearly what?" Laura said confused.

"That picture," I pointed at the photo being projected on the board, "it's blatantly photoshopped, I can tell straight away. If you bumped into her in the street you probably wouldn't even recognise her they've done so much to it, she barely looks human."

Laura continued to look at me completely puzzled as if I was speaking a foreign language.

"So you're saying she doesn't look like that in real life?"

I loaded up a video on YouTube of a model being photographed and then the photo being altered in Photoshop in high speed. As the video was playing I was describing to Laura what was happening and how the image was being manipulated, to highlight the deceptive nature of things like magazine cover photos. She watched as the model's eyes were made bigger and her skin was airbrushed, her hair was lengthened and given more body, her neck and her legs were stretched, her arse was plumped up and her legs and waist were slimmed down, finally the original and the finished product were shown side by side and I paused the video.

"Look now, do you see what I mean? Can you see how fake she looks compared to the original? She was an attractive woman to begin with but they still did all this crap to her, and look at the end she looks all weird and out of proportion. This is part of the reason why, girls in particular, develop all kinds of insecurities and eating disorders, because they want to take photos and look like these models but they don't understand that the models themselves don't even look like that. No one looks like that. The photos are manipulated by some guy on a computer but no celebrity ever admits it. Then girls want to go and get plastic surgery so that they can actually look like these fake people, it's really bad. It's everywhere as well, in men's magazines they do it too, make people's muscles look more defined or give them flawless skin, all sorts of stuff... Do you get what I'm saying?"

I looked at Laura after my rambling rant as she stared at me silently. Contemplating and digesting all of the information she had received, wrapping her head around the reality that was the illusion, she sat frozen silently in her seat. I have just blown her mind, I thought to myself. I am watching the epiphany in real time, she is now awakened, enlightened. I have just unplugged her from the mother fucking Matrix.

"Hmmm, so, err, where can I get a hold of this Photoshop thing then?" She asked.

CHINESE EYES

I was sat in a history lesson working as a TA with a year nine girl called Mel. The teacher, Grant was talking about the Vietnam war and had a rather harrowing image on the board. It was that famous photo of a naked nine-year-old named Kim Phuc and some other children running for their lives from a napalm strike. Grant asked Mel what her first thoughts are upon seeing the image. Mel paused for a moment and looked intensely at the faces of the people in the image.

"How do Chinese people get their eyes like that?"

The room went silent, as we all tried to figure out if we'd misheard her, alas we hadn't.

"Huh?" Grant said, clearly confused.

Mel went on, "I want my eyes to do that, it looks nice."

Now I should add at this point that Grant was not the most professional of people, he could not resist the temptation to mess with the fragile and gullible minds of students in our school. This is a guy who I once witnessed tell students for a laugh, that rabbits shit out raisins and encouraged them to find said raisins and eat them whilst they were getting stoned on the weekend.

"Well just buy new eyes then," he said.

"What d'ya mean?" Asked Mel as she leaned closer.

"Just look on eBay or Amazon, you can get them anywhere really, just search for Chinese eyes and you'll find them."

I could see the excitement building up inside her and I couldn't let it go on any longer, I felt bad.

"Mel, don't listen to him he's having you on."

"What do you mean?" She said.

Grant began to laugh, I decided not to address the fact that Vietnamese people and Chinese people come from completely separate countries and decided to focus on the more pressing issue.

"Mel, you can't just buy new eyes on the internet," I said gently, "their eyes look different, but they are just born like that."

She looked at me all deflated, clearly gutted that her dream of having Chinese eyes was slipping away.

"I don't get it, so I can't have Chinese eyes?"

"No," I replied. "It doesn't work like that Mel it's just the way that they're born. It's like black people, you know, why are they black?"

Mel thought for a moment before she responded.

"I don't know... they drink a lot of coffee?"

IS THAT A TIT WANK?

While working at the PRU I was stood talking in the hallway with another teacher, her name was Fran. She was monitoring the halls as students frequently absconded from lessons and she was on duty to coax them back into class. I had PPA time (Planning, Preparation and Assessment time) but had nothing to do so decided to chat with her and keep her company as it was pretty quiet.

After ten minutes or so one of the students, a year eight boy called Chris, left his classroom and sat in the corner on the floor roughly ten metres from us. This was a regular occurrence and so we said nothing initially. Chris was a very small blonde-haired sweet-looking boy but he had severe anger management issues. At times he was a completely selfish little prick and I'll give an example of that later, but anyway, he was bullied at his previous school quite badly, partly due to his size and seemed hell-bent on ensuring that this would never happen again. As a result, he would act like he was tough and fearless at the slightest sign of trouble as a defence mechanism, he would flip tables, throw chairs and destroy anything in his path if he felt threatened. He would also lash out at staff regularly but then usually end up in tears after his outburst as he was unable to regulate his emotions. Having said all of that he was also hilarious, academically very intelligent beyond his years and at times showed such innocence and vulnerability that you really saw the little boy behind the facade.

A couple of minutes passed and he still had said nothing, he looked annoyed and confused, muttering to himself.

Fran mouthed to me, "What d'ya think, kicked out or walked out?"

I shrugged as I mouthed back, "We're about to find out."

I nodded at Chris and asked, "What's up?"

"That lesson is shit and them lot in there are being annoying." He replied.

"Annoying?" Asked Fran.

"Yeah, and they keep talking about my mom on about that she's all loose and shit."

"Oh!"

"Yeah, and David said she does tit wanks!" He proclaimed while shrugging his shoulders.

I turned away from him holding back the urge to laugh, Fran's eyes were as wide as humanly possible, her lips trembling as she too held back laughter.

"What the fuck's tit wank even mean? Wanking your tits? That doesn't even make sense." Chris said abruptly.

Still trying my hardest not to laugh and trigger a fit of rage from Chris I just shook my head and looked at the floor.

"Don't worry about it mate, David's an idiot."

Chris completely disregarded my comment and proceeded.

"Do you two know what a tit wank is?"

Fran choked out a little laugh but managed to kind of hold it together.

"Ask Mr Foe."

Chris looked at me waiting for me to enlighten him, I thought about it for a second and decided against it.

"Ask your parents when you get home?" I said with a smile.

"No, my mom and dad would batter me, it's obviously something rude. I'm gonna Google it," he said.

"Ok," I responded.

We all stood in silence for the longest and most awkward ten seconds imaginable. Fran and I desperately tried to avoid eye contact with each other knowing that we would erupt into laughter at the slightest glance. Chris rose to his feet with purpose, looked at his chest and then looked at his hands. He had them held so that they made circles like you would do if you were miming using binoculars but at chest height. He then started rapidly moving them back and forth alternately as if he was literally wanking off some imaginary tits. That was it, neither Fran nor I could keep it together any longer we both burst out laughing uncontrollably. Tears streamed down our faces as we looked back and forth from Chris to each other.

"Is that it?!" Chris shouted with excitement, "is that a tit wank?"

I'VE BEEN STABBED!

The deputy headteacher of the school was a fat, lazy woman in her mid-forties. She used to work at quite a fancy mainstream school and banged on about it all the fucking time. She drove a brand new range rover and couldn't get through the morning meeting without mentioning how great it was to drive on the motorway with all its fancy features. She looked down her nose at everyone but in particular the more impoverished students. Her name was Mrs Hope, the irony being that she was completely awful at her job and was quite accurately nicknamed Hopeless.

Hopeless would waddle into her office at the slightest sign of trouble with any of the students to smash chocolate into her face-hole, leaving the rest of the staff to deal with the problem alone. If ever she was forced into a position where she did have to deal with a student's behaviour it was a nightmare, she would no doubt just wind them up and push their buttons before conceding and fleeing back to her office to gorge on more cake and biscuits. Words cannot describe her level of incompetence and one of the students who regularly caused her to demonstrate this was Hayley.

Hayley was in year eleven and had been with us for about a year or two, she was not particularly bright but she had a good heart and really valued friendships. She was very small and could probably have passed for a year eight but my god when she was angry she demonstrated unbelievable strength, like a tiny Hulk. Hopeless really hated Hayley for the simple fact that Hayley regularly, accurately and very publicly called her out for being shit at her job and it was obvious to everyone, as a result, Hayley hated her too.

On this particular day, all of the students had been dismissed from school and I was sat in the staff room with a few other members of staff. After roughly ten minutes one of the students, Mel, returned to school and sat in reception crying, asking for us to call her a taxi because she had just been beaten up by some of the students on the way home.

Mel wasn't making a great deal of sense with her description of what had occurred and to be frank, she looked fine, not a single hair out of place. Mel came from an affluent family and was very spoilt, she came to school every day dressed like she was going on a night out and after receiving the beating she claimed to have received we were baffled as to how she still looked pristine.

I and a few other members of staff headed swiftly down the road hoping to catch the students involved before they escaped on the bus, however to our surprise they were not trying to escape at all, they were actually also on their way back to the school and they were livid, Hayley in particular.

"What's her problem, go on, what's she said the fucking twat?!" Yelled Hayley.

The rest of the students were also ranting about how much Mel talks shit, cries about nothing and was a drama queen.

"We're not entirely sure what's going on, we're hoping you could fill us in," said Jenny.

Jenny was one of the teaching assistants and she, out of all of the staff, had the most positive relationship with Hayley.

"Right," Hayley began, "so we're all walking to the bus stop and we see Mel walking on her own on the other side of the road. She was already crying so I shouted to her asking what was wrong, but she completely blanked me. So then we all walked over the road to her and she literally just chucked her bag on the floor and ran off back to the school saying I'm gonna tell them what you done. I swear on my mom's life yeah, nobody even touched her. I even told everyone not to go through her bag and I have it here, I was bringing it back to the school."

All of the students were adamant that this was the truth and Hayley seemed genuine. We all walked together back to the school to find Hopeless stood in the reception area with Mel and before anybody else could get a word out she started shouting.

"That's it, Hayley, you're excluded for three days, I'm not having you assault people!"

Hayley began protesting her innocence but to no avail. I and the other members of staff began trying to tell Hopeless the other students' version of events but she was not listening in the slightest.

"You'd better leave now before the police are called!" She continued.

"Call them for what, I haven't fucking done anything!" Hayley screamed back.

Hopeless quickly ushered Mel back into the main part of the building and attempted to shut the door on Hayley.

"I hate that girl," muttered Hopeless, "she's horrible."

All of the staff looked at her stunned, we couldn't believe what she had just said in front of all of the students. Having heard this Hayley was understandably further enraged and began yanking at the door. Unable to fully close the door against Hayley's hulk strength, Hopeless blocked the half-opened doorway with her body and clung on to the door as Hayley continued to try to force her way through.

"Let me speak to Mel then if you don't believe me, I haven't fucking touched her!"

Hopeless and Hayley were pushing into one another like rugby players in a scrum, fighting to gain control of the door when all of a sudden Hopeless began to scream.

"Aaaah, I'm being stabbed! I've been stabbed! She stabbed me!"

A confused Hayley, started yelling back, "What the fuck are you on about? Just get out of the way!"

Hopeless shoved Hayley out of the doorway and slammed the door shut.

"I'm calling the police, I've been stabbed," she whimpered and ran into her office.

We all, staff and students stood around absolutely perplexed, we saw no knife, no blood, no anything indicative of a stabbing. Hopeless refused to leave her office until the police arrived which they did pretty quickly. Jenny had managed to calm Hayley down by this point and the two of them sat in the reception area with the other students.

The police came and Hopeless came out of her office clutching her abdomen like Mercutio in his final moments.

"We need to search you, Hayley, can you stand up please?" Asked the officer.

Hayley rose to her feet and handed over her handbag. The two officers began frisking her and routing through her belongings as Jenny explained to them what had gone on in the reception area. After a thorough search, the police had found nothing on her and in the bag they found no knife. They did, however, find a pair of earrings. Upon further inspection, they spotted a small hole where one of the earrings had poked through the side of the handbag.

"She has a knife, I'm certain of it. She must have given it to someone else or thrown it on the roof or something," Hopeless protested.

The officer asked Hopeless to show her the wound that she

was still clutching and we all edged in closer intrigued to see the bloodbath. From the way she was acting you would have expected to see blood pissing out of her abdomen like Mr Orange in Reservoir Dogs, but we were instead struck with the biggest anticlimax in world history.

"Where is the injury?" The officer asked.

"Here!" Hopeless pointed at her blubber, turning her head unable to look at the damage she'd sustained.

"Hmmm, yeah I think I can see a little scratch or something there, it was definitely the earring. It must have poked through the bag as she was trying to push past you at the door."

The students all doubled over with laughter as did the staff, even the police officers struggled to contain their amusement and Hopeless stormed off in a huff to the sound of the students mocking her.

"I've been stabbed! I've been stabbed!" They cried.

IT'S A GOOD JOB
I LIKE YOU

I taught a year ten student called Kingsley, he was a strange character to figure out. He had pretty serious mental health issues and would flip from being a loveable joker to an aggressive, violent uncontrollable force around the PRU once triggered. Everyone at the school knew that his mother was terminally ill with cancer and recognised that this was a part of the reason for his sporadic, unpredictable behaviour and lack of engagement with his work.

Kingsley was very intelligent and if he liked you he was very compassionate and caring. One day for example, when I was in the middle of teaching a lesson I sneezed so hard, the jolt from it caused my neck to go into spasm and I couldn't turn my head, I was in severe pain and could barely move. As ridiculous and slapstick comedy-esqe this scenario was, Kingsley saw the pain that I was in and rushed to get me some help. Most students would have taken this opportunity to fuck with me in one way or another, maybe steal some shit out of my desk, go for a cigarette out the back or at the very least just sit and mock me, but not Kingsley. He sprung out of his seat with his arms flailing and ran as fast as he could down the hallway.

"Jenny! Jenny help! Foe's neck's all fucked up!" He yelled. "Quick time, get him an ice pack or a heat pack or some kind of pack!"

I could hear him running from room to room in a panic.

"Jenny! Where are you? Foe needs first aid!" I heard him shout as he bolted down the corridor.

A few minutes later he and Jenny returned.

"What's wrong with Foe then Kingsley?"

"What's wrong? Look at him his necks all crippled and shit. He needs help!"

As much as I appreciated his concern, his overly dramatic actions were making me laugh, which was making my neck worse and subsequently wince in pain. With each wince, he became more animated with his actions and the cycle continued. Jenny went to get me some pain killers and 'some kind of pack' for my neck, and Kingsley helped me gently into my chair, ensuring that I was ok.

By the end of the lesson, my neck had started to ease up a bit and I was getting some movement back. Before he left the classroom Kingsley walked up to me and placed a hand on my shoulder.

"You alright now Foe?" He said with a smile. "It's a good job I like you y'know or you'd have been stuck like that forever."

A few days later, Kingsley found himself locked in the boy's toilet, he went to take a shit and the lock had broken on the inside of the door. Realising that he was stuck he shouted for help and what seemed like the entire student cohort had coalesced outside the door to laugh at the situation. I must admit it was funny to begin with but after a minute or two claustrophobia began to settle in and Kingsley started to panic. The toilet was basically a cupboard, it wasn't like a cubicle where you could climb over or under the door and his anxiety levels were rising rapidly. Staff managed to get the students back to their classrooms quite swiftly leaving me and Jenny with Kingsley.

Jenny was sat on the floor outside the door talking calmly to Kingsley, trying to refocus his attention on other things while I attempted to open the door from the outside. After another couple of minutes, he again began to panic, he was getting tearful and then started screaming quite frantically.

"Kingsley, I'm going to have to kick the door in ok? You need to get back as far as possible!" I shouted.

Jenny then stood up and out of the way and was also shouting instructions.

"Get as far back from the door as possible Kingsley, Foe's about to kick in the door!"

I stood back and booted the door as hard as I could, and with the sound of the bang and the wood splitting at the lock Kingsley screamed louder, I took a couple of steps backwards ready to go again.

"Get right back!" Jenny shouted.

I charged at the door and kicked it with everything I had. The door flew open and smashed into the wall to reveal Kingsley crouched sideways on top of the toilet lid shielding his face with one arm and clinging onto the cistern with the other. Tears trickled from under his glasses, as he looked at Jenny and me.

"Fucking hell what took you so long?" He said as he wiped a tear from his chin, "I thought I was gonna be smelling that fat stinking shit all day."

I put my hand on Kingsley's shoulder.

"You alright Kings?" I said with a smile. "It's a good job I like you y'know or you'd have been stuck in here forever."

SUPER TEACHER!
DUN-D-D-DUUUURN!

In the morning meeting, there was a new member of staff. She sat up properly in her chair, her back straight and chin up with her hands folded in her lap. She had a slight pout and looked at everyone through her glasses which were, in a cliché fashion, perched on the end of her nose. I hated her instantly.

"I would like to introduce Linda to everyone," Hopeless said with a big smile on her face. "Linda is our new teacher and will be covering for Grant while he's off."

Before anybody could even respond she continued, clearly excited.

"Well, she's going to be covering but also helping to do other stuff with me in the office. Oh, and you too, she'll be popping in to help you all improve your lessons, oh my god she can do everything, she's amazing."

We all started looking around at each other confused. Who the fuck is this woman, Hopeless' fluffer? She can do everything, she's amazing? Fuck my life, what are we then, all fucking useless? I thought. This bitch has been in the building two minutes and all of a sudden she's going to be showing us how to improve our lessons, can't wait, we thought.

My phone started vibrating in my pocket, I checked it to find a WhatsApp message from Kate that said 'Fucking hell it's Super Teacher! Dun-d-d-duuuurn!'. I messaged her back, 'Lmfao I know, Hopeless has climbed right up her arse and set up shop already by the sounds of things.'

Super Teacher then stood up and cleared her throat.

"Hi everyone," she said in her snooty tone, "so, just to touch on what Mrs Hope has said, I don't want you panic or to think that I'm here to tell you all what to do."

We didn't.

"But from discussions that Mrs Hope and I have had, I think that there are many things that I can help to assist with, in terms of teaching and learning and regarding the students' behaviour in lessons." She went on, "I have plenty... of experience. Erm, as I'm sure you all do too, but hopefully I can help make what I'm sure are amazing lessons even more amazing. Thank you."

The room fell silent, WHO...THE FUCK... IS THIS BITCH? Have I missed something? And why is she talking to us all like we're toddlers with this condescending tone? I looked around the room and it was clear that I was not alone in my thoughts. The meeting finished and Super Teacher went to Grant's room to teach her first lesson. She had a year nine group, not the worst group but the year nines, in general, were a bit of a nightmare.

Now I did not witness this part myself as I was in my classroom but apparently, this is how it went. Super Teacher walked into the classroom to find her four year-nine boys already in there, Harvey was sat in the teacher's chair at the front of the room playing music on the laptop. Before she even introduced herself to the students or bothered to try and find out anything about them including their names, she gave Harvey an order.

"Get out of my chair and go sit in your normal chair."

"This is where I always sit actually," Harvey replied

"That's funny, you don't look like a teacher, so come on, up you get," she retorted as she placed her belongings next to the desk.

Kate, sensing that this would end badly, confirmed to Super Teacher that Harvey does in fact sit there every lesson as he likes to control the PowerPoint presentation for Grant.

"Well not anymore, so come on, find another seat," said Super Teacher, again in the most condescending tone ever heard.

Martin, already sick of her, decided he would rather exit via the window than to stay and listen to her bullshit so out he went, meaning Kate had to leave the room to go and get him back.

Roughly thirty minutes into the lesson Kate came to my classroom and slyly handed me a note, as she handed it to me she smiled.

"I think they wanted you in History, I'll watch your class." She smirked.

I left my classroom and took a look at the note which said 'Super Teacher LOL!' I walked round to the classroom where she was teaching and she was stood outside her classroom door with a little note pad and a pen.

"I'm writing down everything you're doing in there," she said.

The students had locked her out of her classroom and barricaded the door shut with tables and chairs, they had music pumping out and we're dancing around rapping to Man's Not Hot by Big Shaq.

"Open the door!" She ordered.

"Say please," came the response.

"I'm not going to say please, you're going to open the door," she said, this time with more conviction.

"Sayyyyy pleeeeease."

She then turned and saw me stood a few metres away.

"It's fine, don't worry I'm writing down everything that they are doing to send to their parents," she smiled attempting to hide her embarrassment.

Why she was writing things down was beyond me, with the type of students that we had, writing things down and sending it home to parents meant fuck all.

"This is your last chance, open the door!" She said as she banged on the door.

The students were laughing hysterically and giving her the middle finger at the window in the door.

"Ooooh last chance or I'll smack your bum bum," they mocked.

She then started attempting to force the door open by pushing into it with her shoulder and panic was beginning to show in her face.

"Do you want some help?" I asked reluctantly.

"No I'm fine, I've dealt with things like this before."

Hopeless then arrived to help her protégé.

"This is Mrs Hope, open the door now! I'm not having this," she whined.

"My handbag is in there and that's my personal property, which you have effectively stolen. Now open the door," moaned Super Teacher.

Now why she told them that her handbag was in the room I have no idea, they clearly hadn't noticed it or did not care about it but drawing attention to it was a foolish thing to do. We all waited in the corridor for a few moments and there was no response. Then a middle finger appeared at the window followed by a room full of laughter.

Lesson time had come to an end and it was time for the groups to move to their next class. I was honestly loving the entire interaction but had my own lesson to get back to so I walked up to the window and looked inside. Harvey was sat in the teacher's chair at the front of the room putting the next song on. I tapped on the glass and got his attention.

"What you saying Foe?" He said with a smile.

"What are YOU saying Harvey, why are you barricaded in?"

"Man, she's a bitch. I always sit in Grant's chair and she's trying to tell me I've gotta move so fuck her enit."

"Yeah I get your point, but listen it's lesson change now anyway so you might as well come out."

"Alright one sec."

It took them a couple of minutes to deconstruct the barricade but during this time there was also a lot of whispering and chuckling from within the room. Eventually, the students all walked out of the room laughing hysterically. Last out of the room was Harvey, who as he walked by Super Teacher stopped for a moment, looked her intensely in the eyes and whispered one of the most disturbing things I have ever heard.

"Smell your phone, bitch."

WATCH WHAT
HAPPENS

Kingsley's mother died on a Sunday night and the next morning he came to school. All of the students knew that she had passed away and for the most part they were very supportive towards him. They hugged him, told him that if there was anything they could do to help they would and he was very appreciative. This from students who were generally considered to be the naughtiest, vilest and most atrocious little bastards in the area. It was really heart-warming to see the levels of compassion and care that they showed.

A day or two later, the staff had decided to put a basket together for Kingsley of things he liked, mainly sweets, chocolate, biscuits and magazines. Kate had wrapped it all up in plastic and tied it with a ribbon so it looked all nice and left it in my classroom. Chris (the tit wanker) saw the huge basket of treats and demanded some sweets from it.

"Gimmie some of them sweets Foe," he said.

"Can't mate sorry, they're not mine they're for Kingsley, from the staff."

"What, just because his mom's died he gets all that? So what. That's not fair."

(Remember before when I told you Chris could be a selfish prick?)

For months after Kingsley's mother died he would occasionally come and sit in my classroom by the door on the floor. Sometimes he'd want to talk, sometimes he just wanted to be left alone to think. He would often talk about how much he missed his mom and how much he wanted to go and live with his aunt, partly because she reminded him of his mother and partly because she cared for him a lot more than his father did.

Staff suspected that Kingsley was been beaten by his father, he had lots of scars on his arms and legs and despite our regular safeguarding referrals nothing seemed to change. I'll never forget when one day his father turned up unannounced at the school in the middle of the day (I knew that he did this from time to time although I hadn't witnessed it myself at this point), the headteacher brought him to my classroom where I was teaching Kingsley and I have never seen such an immediate change in behaviour from a child. Kingsley was instantly compliant, spoke quietly, had his chin to his chest and made minimal eye contact. It was surreal, it was creepy, it was awkward. I felt compelled to show Kingsley's father all of the work that his son had done in my lessons and tell him how well Kingsley does in my classes, hoping that he would say something positive to his almost frozen child or at least smile, but no, he just nodded, said ok and gave Kingsley the death stare.

A few months later a teaching assistant called Darrell came to work at the school and he knew Kingsley's family. To begin with, Kingsley seemed happy to have him at the school and was very quick to tell people that he knew him and even referred to him as 'kind of like my uncle' to begin with, however within a couple of weeks that completely changed. He hated Darrell and hated that he worked at the PRU.

Kingsley told me, Kate and Jenny that Darrell goes to his house daily and reports back to his father everything that he does and says at school no matter how minor, which always lands him in trouble.

One day Kingsley was feeling down about his mother passing away and had kicked off a bit in the morning, he kicked a door and broke the hinge slightly. Jenny had a talk with him and managed to calm him down and cheer him up before she sent him round to my lesson, however by the time Kingsley made it to my classroom he seemed down once again, he sat in the corner with Kate just staring at his work. About a minute later Darrell came to the classroom window and tapped on the glass.

"Is he doing his work?" He said to Kate.

"Yes, we're fine," she replied.

We both thought that it was weird but didn't think much of it, we assumed he was just being nosey as usual. In the staffroom after the lesson Jenny walked in and was clearly upset and annoyed, we asked her what was up and she explained to us that she had just gone and reported something to Liz and felt it was not taken seriously. She then told us that as Kingsley left the room after she had finished talking to him about kicking the door that morning, he came across Darrell in the corridor. She had the door open and clearly heard him say to Kingsley, 'Watch when I come round your house later and tell your Dad everything you've done. Watch what happens.' She then stepped out of the room as Kingsley was walking away and asked Darrell what he meant by that comment and he didn't say anything, he just smirked, shrugged his shoulders and walked away.

THE SNOW DAY
THAT NEVER WAS

One day it had been snowing on the way into work, nothing major but just enough for it to settle on the ground. We were in no danger of snowball fights unless kids were planning on spending half an hour scraping snow together from the entire car park to make one measly ball, but still, nobody really wanted to be in work. It was cold and miserable and we all just wanted to get back into bed.

Jenny, Kate, Grant and I sat in the staffroom complaining about how gutted we were that it hadn't snowed enough for us to get a proper snow day, amid all this Jenny made the following comment.

"Hopeless is running things today, I reckon she's so dumb that if we tell her we're going to get snowed in she'll panic and send us home."

Now keep in mind the following three things. Number one, we had all managed to drive miles to school without any problems, number two, it had already stopped snowing and number three, the amount of snow on the ground was barely the depth of a pound coin. Still, we wanted a snow day and God damn it we were going to get a snow day. We all left the staffroom and sat in the meeting room where Hopeless was preparing for the day, we began talking about how the snow was terrible and how bad it would be if it got worse and snowed even more. We started discussing this entirely hypothetical scenario whereby all of the staff were snowed in with the students and how much trouble it would cause. Hopeless hated the majority of the students because she just could not relate to or manage them and the thought of being trapped in a tiny school with them all was clearly terrifying her. She was getting fidgety and sweating profusely.

"Do you think it's going to get that bad then?" She interjected nervously.

We all gave neutral responses but then immediately continued to talk as though we knew, one hundred per cent, that as soon as the students got into the building an avalanche of snow was going to descend upon the school like some kind of biblical apocalyptic blizzard, destroying all communication devices within a twenty-five-mile radius and inevitably result in cannibalism as we fight to survive like the movie Alive.

The rest of the staff trickled into the meeting room as Hopeless shuffled nervously in her chair. Once everyone had arrived Hopeless began.

"Right then everybody, before we get started, there has been a slight change of plans for today, I don't think that this snow is going to let up."

Remember it had already stopped snowing at this point.

"It's pretty bad out there and will only get worse."

There was literally less than half a centimetre of snow on the ground and to reiterate, IT HAD ALREADY STOPPED SNOWING.

"Carol, I'm going to need you to call all of the parents and tell them not to send their children into school. We are only going to be in for half the day today so teachers just get your marking and planning up to date and then go, TAs speak to teachers and see if any jobs need doing."

Oh my God, we fucking did it, we thought to ourselves, this fucking idiot actually took the bait. Carol left immediately to start calling parents and tell them not to send their children into school whilst we all sat in the meeting avoiding eye contact with one another, a few minutes later the meeting ended and we all went into the staffroom and exploded into a mad laughing frenzy. We basically had the morning as PPA, and then we were going home at twelve, we were elated and could not believe what we had pulled off, we pretty much Derren Brown mind-fucked her and it felt good, I mean fair enough it was half a day, not the whole day but bloody hell having no students in and doing a couple of hours' work was pretty good going.

At about ten o'clock I was sat in my classroom and I could hear Jenny and Kate in the TA's office laughing but kind of nervously, so I went in to see what was going on.

"What are you two laughing about?"

"Have you looked outside?" They said in unison

Oh great I thought, we've tempted fate and now we're actually going to get snowed in. I looked out of the window and saw nothing. As in no snow at all. It had completely melted away and there was barely a puddle in the ground, not a snowflake in sight. Staff all over the building could not help but laugh at what had gone on especially when we told them how the plan was hatched and executed.

By eleven o'clock it was clear that Hopeless had realised that she'd completely fucked up, parents would be well within their rights to complain and put her in a very awkward situation with Liz and the local authority. I mean giving parents a call at half-past eight in the morning and telling them not to send their kids in because of the impending snowstorm, when half of them were probably driving in it at the time and had to turn back. Not only was she preventing the students from coming in but she was also giving the staff a half-day on full pay and then the icing on the cake, there is not a fucking snowflake anywhere to be seen, I bet they'd have loved it.

Hopeless was frantically pacing around the building looking out of every window she could find just praying to see some snow, and with each clear bit of road and pavement she saw, her hand nervously tapped her thigh, she would then return to her office grab some chocolate digestives and head to another classroom and again look out of the window as if the weather might have changed dramatically between the Maths classroom and the English classroom.

A few minutes before twelve o'clock another meeting was called by Hopeless. Now I have sat in too many pointless meetings to count but this one was something else. It was abundantly clear that she was trying to keep everyone there as long as possible and treat it like some sort of impromptu teacher training day to have some kind of justification for what she had done, she literally invented talking points for the meeting as she went. I honestly can't even remember what they were because they were that ridiculous, nobody cared, nobody participated everyone just wanted to go home.

At the end of the meeting Grant shouted 'Oh look it's snowing again!' and I've never seen her so excited, she looked at the window so fast I'm surprised she didn't get whiplash, alas he was kidding, but the look of absolute heartbreak when she realised it wasn't snowing was totally worth it.

ROAD RAGE

Grant and I were taking the key stage four students on a trip to the apprenticeship exhibition. I never mind going on trips usually, I tended to find that the students acted up a bit, but generally speaking, when they were out in public they behaved better. I guess that it was at least to some degree because they knew that staff would not or could not step in and save them if they got into any serious trouble. Grant, on the other hand, hated trips because he always had to drive the minibus, the students' behaviour on the minibus was awful and he found the students extremely embarrassing when out in public, especially because he'd often be mistaken for one of their dads.

On the way there the students were already hyped up, not because of the idea of getting an apprenticeship but simply because they were not doing their usual lessons. They had been lauding it up to the key stage threes from the moment they got to school and the very idea of going on the minibus somewhere out of school was enough to create pandemonium. There were however one or two students who knew they were as academically intelligent as a bag of rocks, had poor social skills and were understandably very anxious about talking to new people about apprenticeship opportunities. One such student was Bobby, who unless he could somehow get an apprenticeship testing new indica and sativa blends at De Rockerij in Amsterdam had a better chance of winning the national lottery with a bus ticket.

On our way there we stopped at a petrol station to fill up the minibus, Grant filled the tank and went into the shop to pay. I was sat in the front stopping the students from messing with the radio and whatever else was within their reach. A minute later Grant came out of the shop at lightning speed and was absolutely furious.

"What the fuck are you doing!" He shouted. "Are you really that fucking stupid?!"

I was perplexed, who is he talking to and what is he shouting about? I wondered. Well, unbeknownst to me Bobby had decided to get off of the minibus and smoke a cigarette. He was sat on the minibus step in the middle of a petrol station casually puffing on a Richmond.

"Put that out before you kill us all you stupid twat!" Grant balled.

"Yeah chill, two secs" Bobby replied, "I'm almost done."

Grant snatched the cigarette from Bobby's hand and put it out. I turned around and looked at the rest of the students sat in the back.

"Didn't anybody notice that Bobby had jumped off of the

bus and was smoking a cigarette?"

To which the reply I got from Paul was, "Yeah but c'mon it's hardly gonna start a fire really is it? Stop being such a pussy."

Paul was a relatively new student and nobody really liked him, it was pretty obvious why after spending an hour with the boy. He was a spoilt little rich boy who just couldn't help but brag to everyone how much stuff he was given by mommy and daddy, half of the time it was massively over-exaggerated bullshit, like how his mom was going to give him one hundred thousand pounds for his eighteenth birthday, or how he had been offered a spot in a premier league football team but then had to turn it down because he was too young. It seemed to me like his parents had told him how amazing he was for that long that he genuinely believed he was the greatest thing to walk the planet. He was often spotted checking himself out in windows, ensuring that his hair wasn't out of place and was forever looking at designer clothes on the internet. He'd then spend the lesson telling everybody what he was going to buy, before expressing the dilemma that he was running out of space in his walk-in wardrobe... Fucking hell he was annoying.

So, we got to the NEC and it was pretty uneventful, a few of the students actually took it seriously and tried to get information about apprenticeships that they were interested in, but the few students that I was walking around with decided that they would rather hang out by the TARDIS (which seemed like an odd thing to have at the apprenticeship show) and photobomb people who were taking photos in front of it. They would casually stroll into the view of the camera while people were posing, stand dead straight like a soldier, with a poker face, their eyes as wide as possible and of course subtly throwing up a middle finger at waist height.

On the way home, Paul heard about the photobombing that the other students were doing and thought it was hilarious, wanting to get in on the action he decided he would start giving the finger to people driving alongside us on the dual carriageway. One of the people he did this to was a man, about forty, driving a white van and he clearly was not in the mood to be flipped off by a fifteen-year-old boy on a school trip. The man drove ahead of the minibus and then pulled across both lanes blocking the road before slamming on his brakes. He then jumped out of his van leaving the door wide open and started shouting at a very confused Grant.

"Fucking big man are you? Get out here then!" The man raged

"What? What are you talking about?" Said Grant.

"Him there," he pointed at Paul, "giving me the middle finger, I'll fucking chin ya right now!"

Paul sunk down in his seat immediately.

"Look mate, I dunno what they did but they're a bunch of school kids, they act like prats. None of 'em are gonna fight ya. Can you just move your van so I can get 'em back to school please?"

The enraged van driver continued to threaten everyone but mainly Paul for a minute or two while the students sat in utter silence like it was remembrance day. My two favourite threats that he made were, 'I'll rip your face off and make you eat it', amazing visuals on that one, and 'I'll kick your fucking tiny balls out son'. That's right out, not in or off but out. I assume this entails kicking the testicles so hard that they rip out of the scrotum... ouch.

Eventually, the man got back in his van and drove off and as soon as we got moving again Paul's mouth opened.

"Fucking dickhead, he's lucky I didn't knock him out."

And with that comment Grant completely lost it and he slammed his foot down on the brake, half of the students who weren't wearing their seatbelts flew off of their seats into the back of the seat in front of them. Traffic once again was backing up behind us and people were beeping their horns but Grant had to get something off of his chest, he unclipped his seatbelt and turned around.

"Oh ok, you were going to knock him out were you? Funny that, because you didn't say shit when he was stood there ready to smash your damn face in. You're all a bunch of pussies! Shouting your mouths of all the fucking time but then when someone calls you out on your shit, look at you, eh, look. Not one of you said a bloody word, so save the 'he's lucky I didn't knock him out' bit Paul. I should have opened the bastard door and let him drag you off the fucking minibus you little cunt." He then turned back around to face forward, looked at the students in the rearview mirror and said, "And I'll tell you now, I wouldn't have stepped in, I'd have let him fucking cripple you. Now put your fucking seatbelt on and shut the fuck up."

Needless to say, the rest of the journey back to school was relatively quiet.

OWEN WANTS
HIS PHONE

There's really no nice way to say this but Owen was born with fetal alcohol syndrome and as a result, had an abnormal appearance which is generally symptomatic of this condition. He was very short and scrawny, his head was small, his lips were extremely thin especially his upper lip and he had very small eye sockets. His eyesight was terrible so he wore glasses with lenses thick enough to stop bullets and his coordination was also noticeably poor. Couple this with ginger hair, the complexion of milk and angry adolescent acne, and as you probably assumed Owen got bullied quite badly in his previous school.

The bullying Owen received caused him to not attend school regularly all the way up until year ten when he joined us, and with his diminished brain development because his mother regularly decided to polish off a couple of bottles of Zinfandel whilst pregnant, as you might have guessed his intelligence was way below average. Owen had serious behavioural problems, mental health problems and learning difficulties when he arrived at the PRU and was a known self-harmer. Despite his back story, Owen got on well with both the staff and students at the PRU, he'd made some positive friendships and was attending regularly. He was a really nice boy, he was helpful to others and was always polite to staff, yes he fucked about from time to time of course, but generally, he tried hard to achieve something during his time at the PRU.

One day Darrell came to work wearing a tight shiny shirt with his top two buttons undone and all of the students thought it was hilarious. As you might have expected they immediately started to make fun of him and to be frank so did most of the staff. He must have been working out and thought he'd throw on a fitted shirt to get Liz moist between the thighs before one of their not so secret rendezvous or something, who knows? But whatever the reason was, he was getting shit from the kids all day.

Owen, obviously wanting to fit in, decided to get in on the fun and made some jokes about Darrell's tight shirt. Now, I can't remember exactly what Owen said to Darrell but it was definitely no worse than what many other students and staff (including myself) had said already. It was something about him wasting his time wearing his fitted shirt for Liz because she wasn't coming into school today (she was 'working from home') like I said others had made far more scathing comments. Anyway, whatever it was Darrell decided that he needed to make an example of somebody and was going to send Owen home for his behaviour. Feeling unfairly treated (which he was) Owen sat in the reception area sulking as he waited for Darrell to get his phone from the office. Whilst sat there Maggie, one of the admin staff was chatting to Owen through the reception window and trying to make him feel better as he was very upset about being sent home.

Darrell arrived with Owen's phone, he stood in front of Owen less than a metre away with his arms crossed and puffing out his chest.

"What are you crying for Owen?"

"I'm not crying," Owen said, sat on the chair looking at the floor.

"Could have fooled me, you look like you're crying." Darrell continued.

"I'm not crying. I just want my phone." Owen said as he stood up and held out his hand.

"I'm not crying I just want my phone," Darrell said in a mocking tone, "not got anything else to say?" Darrell asked aggressively.

Owen looked at Maggie who was watching them through the reception window.

"Miss, will you just tell him to give me my phone please so I can go home?"

"Don't talk to her, I'm talking to you." Darrell said as he inched closer to Owen.

Owen took a step back while looking down at the floor, he

glanced up through his thick lenses and slowly reached to take his phone from Darrell's hand but Darrell quickly pulled the phone away from Owen's reach and held it high in the air. Maggie who was watching the entire interaction could see Owen was clearly upset, being humiliated and felt intimidated. She slid the glass window open and interjected.

"Darrell, what are you doing? Just give him the phone so he can go."

"I'm giving him the phone, one minute."

Owen slowly stretched out a trembling hand as he once again reached for his phone and once again Darrell pulled the phone away.

"I'll give you the phone in a minute. Wait!"

Magnified tears started to slowly trickle down Owen's cheeks and he turned to face the wall.

"You see, what you crying about? What's wrong Owen am I annoying you? Huh? See it's not nice when someone messes you about is it?" Darrell said with a smirk.

"I just want my phone so I can go home!"

Owen kicked the door open and stomped outside, clutching his hair in both hands. Maggie looked on in shock as Owen paced up and down outside the front of the building in tears.

"Fucking wanker!" He yelled before punching the wall as hard as he could. "I just want to go home; I just want to go home!"

Owen sobbed as he continued to smash his fist into the

brick wall. Maggie immediately got up from her desk and ran out of the office round to where Darrell was stood.

"Give me that phone now!" She demanded.

Maggie swiped the phone from Darrell's hand before he even had a chance to respond, she ran outside and placed her hand on Owen's shoulder.

"It's ok sweetie, here look I've got your phone for you."

"I just want my phone so I can go home." Owen whimpered.

"I know sweetie, look, here look I have your phone here in my hand."

Maggie waved the phone in front of Owen's face and he wiped the tears from his cheeks leaving a smear of blood across his face from his hands.

"Come inside Owen, I'll get you a drink and we can clean you up a bit yeah? What d'ya think, would you like a cup of tea?"

Owen nodded and Maggie walked him into the office. Darrell at this point had now fucked off and was in Liz's office on the phone to her attempting to cover his own arse before the shit hit the fan. As Maggie walked Owen into the office Jenny was walking down the corridor.

"Oh Jenny, you're a first aider aren't you? Can you come and have a look at Owen's hand please?"

Jenny walked into the office and took one look at Owen's hand, it was a mess.

"That's broken, he needs to go to A&E right now, let me go grab my keys."

Jenny left immediately to get her keys and drove Owen to the hospital.

The next morning Liz informed us that Darrell had called her from the school shortly after the incident to let her know that Owen had 'gotten a bit upset', had 'overreacted' and had 'a bit of an accident' but that everything was fine. She told us that the incident had been dealt with and was no longer a cause for discussion. To make things worse she also threw in some victim-blaming stating that Owen should not have even been on the school grounds as he had been told to go home, conveniently skipping over the fact that he wanted to go home but his phone was being held hostage by Darrell.

When the students arrived at school that morning we asked if anybody had heard from Owen, his best friend told us that he had broken bones in three places on his hand.

PAR-TY BUS!

I used to have to drive a minibus to go and collect students from the PRU and to take them for one to one key working sessions. I was supposed to be going and collecting a year eleven girl named Sarah. She was a lovely girl, a little troubled but very mature and down to earth.

Sarah's best friend at the PRU was a ginger boy also in year eleven called Carl, they had been good friends before attending the PRU and their friendship grew stronger each day. Carl never wanted to be in school and would frequently find opportunities to escape from the building, especially when Sarah was not there with him. Carl was never one to miss an opportunity to fuck about and have a laugh, he was very charismatic and cheeky and had this unbelievable ability to draw people into his mischievous antics like a magnet.

Every week I would go to collect Sarah and without fail every week Carl would sneak into the minibus. Some way, somehow no matter how carefully I tried to avoid it he would find a way on, and once he was on, I could not get him off. One time he got on the minibus and lay down in the back, and I had no idea. After an hour and a half session with Sarah, I decided to treat us both to a McDonald's and as I pulled up at the drive-through and was giving our order, from nowhere I heard.

"Yo! I beg you get me a double cheese and chocolate milkshake. Man are starving back here still."

Since that day I always double-checked the minibus before heading off. As he now knew that I checked the minibus thoroughly before driving away, his new thing to do was to get on the minibus and beep the horn. This was like a signal to the rest of the students as they would come stampeding out of the centre and Carl would let them on the bus. Once they were on the bus, it turned into a rave, the music would be blasted out at full volume and they all started jumping about singing and dancing.

One week, in particular, there was just no staff around to help me, I don't know where they were or what they were doing but they certainly were not helping me to control the mayhem that was ensuing, I got off the bus and started calling for help, but nobody came. I had no idea what to do next so I got back on the bus and sat in the driver's seat. I sat for about ten seconds while the students were going crazy all around me dancing to Kid Cudi vs Crookers – Day 'n' Night, it was ridiculously loud, the bus was literally rocking side to side, people in the houses nearby were staring at me in disbelief. I abruptly turned the music right down, turned around in my chair and looked at the students with the death stare. Immediately they all went quiet. There were around fifteen faces crammed into a small minibus just staring at me in silence, waiting for me to go ballistic at them...Then I thought, fuck it, if you can't beat 'em join 'em. I cranked the volume up full blast and sang as loud as I could.

"The lonely loner seems to free his mind at night! At, at, at night!"

Then I started going nuts, fist-pumping the air, bouncing in my seat and joining in the madness. The students burst out laughing and immediately started dancing again whilst chanting in unison.

"PAR-TY BUS! PAR-TY BUS! PAR-TY BUS!"

YOU CAN SEE IT
FROM A MILE AWAY

A new year ten girl started called Amber. On her first day, I did not have her until the final lesson so although I had heard little bits about her our paths had not crossed until she arrived at my classroom.

My first impression when I saw her was that she looked like she'd just walked off of the set for one of the ever-increasingly braindead reality TV shows. She was very skinny, wore high heels, fake hair extensions, fake eyelashes, fake tan, and had a face full of makeup, I think the technical term for the volume of makeup on her face is 'a shit load!'. I don't know what she actually looked without all this fraudulent shit on but I do know that the boys all thought she was 'fire'. I have to say though that this was probably also because on her bottom half she was wearing what seemed to me to be a pair of slightly thicker than average black tights and nothing else... No skirt... No shorts... Just tights. Apparently, they weren't tights they were thin leggings but whatever you want to call them, one thing you definitely could not call them was opaque. They were see-through and I mean blatantly see-through from a distance. It wasn't even like something you had to try to spot, it was instantly noticeable, not to mention the fact that she was wearing a bright pink thong which again could be seen from a mile away.

Amber walked into my classroom with the rest of her group, I introduced myself and set the class their task for the day. As it was her first day I didn't know anything about her and she didn't know me, and being a male teacher I thought it's probably best I don't mention the translucency of her tights masquerading as leggings right now, especially in a classroom full of students. I didn't think it was appropriate and I didn't know how she would react, the last thing I wanted was to embarrass her, upset her, or piss her off during our first encounter. Also, I was thinking to myself surely someone has said something already, she can't have gone through the whole day without another member of staff at least giving her a heads up. How did neither Liz nor Hopeless spot this when they were on the front door this morning welcoming students? I thought to myself. I decided to let it go for now and to mention it at the end of day meeting as there were only forty-five minutes of the school day left.

The meeting started and we were discussing students' behaviour and work throughout the day when someone mentioned Amber. Everybody was talking about what a good day she had, how polite she was and how hard she worked, which was all good and true but I could not believe that not one person mentioned the denier of the fabric over her derriere. Then it came to my turn to talk.

"How on earth she was allowed to make it all the way through the day in those tights or leggings or whatever they were is beyond me. She should not have been allowed to come into school in those if you ask me."

"What do you mean?" Came the response from multiple people in the room.

"What do I mean? Are you all taking the piss? I mean you could see straight through her leggings to her underwear that's what I mean."

I was gobsmacked. I began looking around at everyone just waiting for someone to concur, I knew it was an awkward position to find yourself in as a member of staff admitting that you could see a student's thong and arse cheeks but there was no way in hell that nobody else noticed, they were clearly just reluctant to admit it.

Grant then added "Yeah you could see straight through them, he's right"

Then Liz came out with possibly the most infuriating statement ever uttered in my direction.

"It's funny how the men noticed her see-through leggings isn't it?" Then started giggling.

Darrell and Hopeless, always wanting to be in the boss's good books also started chuckling along with her. All three of them looked at me like they were either waiting for me to laugh too or expecting me to confirm with them that I was some kind of pervert.

"Hang on a minute, what the fuck are you trying to insinuate there?" I said abruptly.

The room went silent. I was so pissed off that I didn't even allow her to respond.

"So what, nobody else noticed all day that you could see straight through to her bare arse? That's bullshit. She had on see-through fucking leggings and a pink thong. End of the day, this is a school full of vulnerable, at-risk children and she's how old? Fourteen? Fifteen? And on her very first day because I'm not a fucking blind idiot I highlight what is potentially a massive safeguarding issue and I'm being looked at like some kind of fucking nonce."

"No, no I didn't mean that I was just saying..., I mean of course it's a serious issue." Liz blurted out.

"Maybe if someone was checking uniform properly in the morning, she wouldn't have made it all the way through to the last lesson with her fucking bare arse on display." Once again there was silence, "Seriously am I the only person who thinks this is a problem that actually needs addressing?"

All of a sudden other members of staff began admitting that they noticed her see-through leggings and Hopeless, who was the designated safeguarding lead, realising that she'd fucked up yet again rushed off to call Amber's parents and tell her to wear more appropriate clothes to school. Ironically covering her own arse... The rest of the meeting went awkwardly on.

SUE KNOWS WHAT SHE HEARD

The food technology teacher was a woman in her late fifties called Sue, she was a bit erratic at times but was undoubtedly at the school for the right reasons. She loved working with the students and was very passionate about her subject. Pretty much every student in the school liked her and respected her. Sue kind of reminded me of Louis Theroux in the way that she interacted with the students. She liked to come across to them as a bit of a naïve airhead and therefore the students would let their guard down around her a little more. She also saw herself as a sort of mother figure or nan to many of the students and to be honest, she probably was to some of them.

In one of her lessons, Tyler and Carl were making pancakes, now I should probably mention at this point that these two boys were major stoners and judging by their eagerness to make the pancakes and subsequently demolish them, I'd say that they had certainly been passing the dutchie 'pon di left-hand side during the lunch break. Whilst burying another stack of pancakes in Nutella, Tyler began chatting to Carl about the hybrid herb they'd just partaken in. Now I wasn't there for this particular conversation but from what I was told, read and know of the students involved, six bucks and my left nut says it went exactly like this.

Tyler - "That cro was loud fam, my head's fucking moggin."

Carl - "Trust me bruv, I'm a half seized still."

Tyler - "Where'd you cop dat?"

Carl - "Some next donny up by my ends enit, he had a crop on."

Tyler - "Ah seen, he had a crop on. You should cop a key from him and shot it. I know a bag of man that would link up for sales still. You'll make bare P."

Carl - "I hollered him still but he ent on it, he just passed me a baller cause I've known him from back-a-day. He just has it for persies really."

Tyler - "Yo, you know who reckons they can get nice ozzes for cheap? Darrell."

Carl - "Fuck off fam, that's pure gas."

Tyler - "Swear down, I put it on my marj. That's what he's saying, go check him."

Which in standard English roughly translates to the following conversation.

Tyler - "That cannabis is very strong, I'm extremely high."

Carl - "I know mate, I'm pretty high too."

Tyler - "Where did you get it from?"

Carl - "A man who lives in my local area, he was growing it."

Tyler - "Oh I understand now, he's growing it. You should buy a kilogram from him a sell it. You'll make a lot of money."

Carl - "I asked him already but he wasn't interested, he just gave me a few grams because I've known him for a long time. He just wants to smoke it himself really."

Tyler - "Do you know who claims they can get nice ounces of cannabis cheap? Darrell."

Carl - "No way mate, that's a complete lie."

Tyler - "I swear on my mother's life, that's what he said. Go and ask him."

After hearing this conversation Sue did not speak to the boys about it, she just logged what she had heard on the schools safeguarding and reporting system immediately after the lesson. She had planned to speak privately with Liz about it at the end of the day, however, by the time we'd reached the staff meeting at the end of the day Liz had already read the log and decided to pull the boys out of their last lesson for a meeting with her and Darrell.

The instant the end of day staff meeting started Liz eagerly reported back to us all that Sue was mistaken, we were told that the boys said the name Darren and not Darrell and that it was nothing to worry about as they had 'handled it'. Now at this point, Sue had not actually told anybody what she heard in the lesson and therefore the rest of the staff team were slightly confused but not particularly suspicious, Sue however, was clearly pissed off. She was sat sideways in her chair with her arms crossed and stared intensely into Liz's soul out of the corner of her eye like Liz had just turned up to her 50th birthday party and took a shit on her cake.

After the meeting, I went and spoke to Sue and she explained to me what had happened. Sue was adamant that she knew what she had heard and was pretty annoyed that the boys had been spoken to by Liz about it but that nothing was said to her or asked of her about the situation. What we found the most unbelievable however was that the meeting that Liz had with Carl and Tyler involved Darrell, the very person they claimed was offering to sell them drugs.

WHA'GWAN
LIKKLE MAN

Carl was tall, skinny, ginger and had spots all over his face, and he wore that look with pride. He was the funniest kid I've ever had the pleasure of teaching by a mile and despite the havoc he reeked around the school, he was a kind and good-hearted boy. For a long time, he was the only year eleven boy in the school and therefore was the top boy by default. If in the same situation most, if not all of the other boys I have taught at the PRU would see this as a green light to intimidate the younger students and act like they were some kind of God among mere mortals, however, Carl was different. He was more like a big brother to the younger students, yes he was a little heavy-handed and threatening at times, but he would make sure they were respectful to staff (the staff that he liked anyway) and tell them to go to their lessons if they were messing about in the corridors.

Despite regularly policing the younger students and ensuring they did as they were told, Carl did almost no work himself in my lessons or anybody else's, but because he was so hilarious he kind of got away with it. It was difficult to keep him on track with his work when he's got you crying with laughter. I would say things to him seriously and sternly and he would always figure out a way to make me laugh and distract me from my original point.

Every day he would ring the school at about 9:10am and ask to speak to Natalie the Behaviour Support Manager. The conversation would undoubtedly always begin with Carl explaining that he's running late but is on his way in, and end with him asking her to make him a cup of tea so he can 'down it quick time' before he goes to his first lesson.

Every time I saw Carl around the school or when he would turn up to my lesson he would do exactly the same thing, he'd start by squaring up to me on his tiptoes and looking me up and down (even though I was still taller than him). He'd then attempt to kiss his teeth which never ever turned out quite right and say 'Wha'gwan likkle man' in the worst Jamaican accent ever. If ever I couldn't find him, I could be ninety-nine per cent certain that he was on the school roof vaping or smoking a cigarette and sunbathing.

On this particular day, Carl arrived at my classroom door wearing a pair of white shutter shades, the English teacher's brown waistcoat over his hoodie and carrying a laptop on his shoulder like a boom box blasting out 212 by Azealia Banks featuring Lazy Jay. He knocked on my classroom door and looked me up and down as I walked to the door to let him in. I opened the door and instantly began to laugh. Carl attempted to kiss his teeth at me but failed miserably as he always did.

"What's so funny likkle man?" He asked.

"Is that John's waistcoat?" I replied.

"It was... it's mine now enit."

He strolled into the classroom and sat in his usual seat, I was just about to tell him to turn the music off when he closed the laptop put his hand on his forehead and shook his head slowly, he had the most disappointed look on his face.

"What's up with you?" I asked with caution and concern.

"Ahh, fucking hell man," he murmured as he continued to slowly shake his head. "This generation is done for Foe, I mean seriously. Look at this shit. Mans can't even spell bitch properly 'round here."

He then pointed to a small bit of graffiti on the desk that said 'Miss Hope is a bich'. As we laughed the headteacher, Liz, turned up with the other two year elevens Sarah and Gina. The two girls sat down and Liz asked to speak to Carl in her office. Approximately ten minutes later Carl came back to the classroom and was pretty pissed off, he walked in and grabbed his shutter shades from off of the desk.

"I'm off Foe, getting excluded again ent I," he said

He then began to take off John's waistcoat, as he did so Darrell came to the classroom door.

"I need to borrow Carl sir," he said abruptly.

Before I could respond Carl flew off the handle.

"Fuck you! I don't wanna talk to you! You're a fucking pagan!"

Darrell attempted to put a hand on Carl's shoulder but it was quickly shrugged off.

"Get off me ya dickhead, you're a fucking pagan, fucking snake bruv," he said as he left the room.

Later on in the day I went and spoke to Grant who informed me that Carl was sent home and excluded because he had come to school with cannabis in his bag and that Darrell had been the one to discover it and report it.

FUCK YOU JENNY!

It was the end of a ridiculously chaotic day, students had been running wild all over the school and causing havoc. Staff were exhausted and eagerly wanted to go home but we were also utterly pissed off because once again Hopeless had failed to clear the lowest bar in managerial history.

Hopeless was supposedly running things on this particular day because once again Liz was not in. Where was Liz? Well, apparently she was 'working from home', which are words that no other headteacher has ever uttered before 3pm in the history of education, because it is nonsensical, and clearly something she conjured from out of her anal cavity one day when she decided that she couldn't be arsed to come to work and do her fucking job. How can I say that with such confidence, maybe because she was the head of a PRU and not a fucking freelance architect! Anyway, digression aside, Hopeless was in charge and as usual, she was putting minced beef in the trifle.

There were several issues raised by various members of

staff during the meeting and as always ninety-nine per cent of it, when you traced back the root of the problem it came grinding to a halt at Hopeless' door. Most notably she had fucked up the timetable and completely missed out an entire class of kids. When it was brought to her attention that four students were wandering around the centre not knowing who's lesson they were supposed to be in, rather than sort it out properly and figure out where they were supposed to be she just started telling pupils whatever they wanted to hear for them to leave her alone.

News that Hopeless was basically letting students do what they wanted for the day spread from student to student like chlamydia in the Playboy Mansion, and soon the entire cohort was out of control. There were so many kids at her door you'd have thought it was Halloween, and in her unwavering idiocy she was telling students that they could swap groups for the day and move to another class for some shit-for-brains reason. Even more unbelievably she told some of them to 'figure it out for themselves', resulting in teachers all of a sudden having students in their lesson that they had no work prepared for. There were also students in classes together who just simply could not focus on work when in the same room, there were students in the same classes that created safeguarding issues and to top it all off there were students who decided they didn't have a lesson and would instead run around causing mayhem, it was a complete fucking mess.

At the end of day meeting when all of these things were highlighted Hopeless did nothing but try to dodge the concerns entirely, handle them in a manner that was counterproductive and even had the audacity to try and blame other members of

staff for her shit show. As you might expect all of this was causing more and more members of staff to get pissed off and vocal
about her lack of common sense. Amidst the understandable
outrage from staff, Darrell was once again attempting to lick
the shit-stained arse of management by jumping to Hopeless'
defence any and every time she began floundering with her responses or had a massive spotlight aimed directly at her incompetence. 'We don't need to discuss this now. People should talk
to Mrs Hope in her office after the meeting about this,' was a line
that left Darrell's mouth numerous times as Hopeless froze like a
deer in headlights.

After the meeting, Jenny walked into the computer room
to complete some work. I was stood at my desk and Darrell was
at the classroom door asking for some paperwork that I had for
him. As I searched for the paperwork on my desk Jenny decided
to question Darrell's motives.

"Darrell, I've got to ask, why are you always so quick and
eager to defend management when staff have genuine issues
and reasons for their comments?"

Darrell took his hands from his pockets and crossed them
in front of his chest.

"I'm not defending her. I just don't think that it was fair
that everyone was ganging up on her." Darrell responded swiftly.

"Nobody was ganging up on her," Jenny explained, "the fact
of the matter is that there are staff who have been here for a long
time and have been trying to sort out certain issues with her,
and we get pissed off when she doesn't take responsibility for the

shit she causes..."

Darrell put his palm up gesturing to stop and interrupted Jenny mid-sentence.

"No look, if everyone is saying stuff and having a go then she's gonna feel like she's been targeted."

"Darrell, she's a grown woman, she can defend herself," she said as she pulled out her chair and sat down.

Darrell then starting rambling, denying that he was defending Hopeless at all, proclaiming that he just thought that what people were saying was not something that should be said in front of everybody else. Always being one to call someone out on their bullshit, Jenny told Darrell in no uncertain terms that it seemed to her that all he was doing was trying to keep everyone from saying things in the meeting that might make Hopeless look bad. By this point, I had sorted out the paperwork for Darrell so I handed it to him and began gathering my things from my desk so that I could head home.

"I just don't get it," Jenny said with frustration. "You should be defending the kids here, but instead you back the wrong horse all the time and it's a joke."

Darrell was still stood in the doorway with his foot on a chair, he had his head down and was muttering something to himself. Jenny who was still sat at the back of the room stood up to see him muttering and then glanced at me with a look of confusion as to what Darrell was mumbling to himself, I couldn't make out a word he was saying and so I just shrugged. After a few more seconds of hearing the muttering Jenny spoke up again.

"If there is something that you want to say, Darrell, just talk," she said.

Darrell then turned and walked out of the classroom, he took about three or four paces before stopping abruptly, he then turned back around to face the classroom pointed directly at Jenny and started screaming like some kind of unhinged psychopath.

"FUCK YOU JENNY! FUCK YOU JENNY!"

Spit flew from his lips as his arms flailed in a frenzy.

"Fuck you Jenny! Yeah?! Fuck you!"

Darrell marched into my classroom and threw his keys and his papers down on the floor.

"Who do you think you're talking to?!" He yelled as he pointed aggressively in her face. "Don't think you can talk to me like that! Fuck you Jenny!"

Hearing the shouting, other members of staff began to arrive at my classroom en masse. There were people everywhere and everyone was talking at once either telling Darrell to calm down or to leave but he continued.

"You make comments all the time in the staff room Jenny and I'm sick of it!" He ranted.

Jenny who up until now had not moved an inch said in the same calm and direct tone,

"I'm just an honest person and if I see you doing stuff I don't agree with I'd rather tell you directly to your face and not talk about you behind your back."

Darrell continued to boil over with anger and was attempting to get closer to Jenny but was being blocked by multiple members of staff. All of the staff were telling him to leave and were clearly worried that he might try to physically assault her, as he was trying to get around them and still shouting, swearing and pointing at her aggressively.

During the shouting, it was a bit difficult to hear all that was said but at one point I clearly heard Darrell call Jenny unprofessional. I think the irony and hypocrisy was too much for her to handle and Jenny then completely flipped.

"How can you call ME unprofessional?!" She yelled with fury.

She then started listing students' names and counting on her fingers, those with whom Darrell had shown extreme levels of unprofessionalism whilst dealing with them.

"Kingsley, Owen, Paul, Carl! Do I need to continue?! Tyler, Gina..."

By now the room was in complete chaos, people were telling Jenny to calm down and telling Darrell to leave as he was still trying to push past people to get to her. Bodies were jostling around everywhere and everybody was shouting, it was mayhem. After a couple of minutes of that, Darrell left and a few members of staff followed him to ensure he left the premises. A minute later Katherine returned.

"Are you ok Jenny? You should just go home if you want to go," she said.

"No I'm fine thanks, Kath, I'm gonna stay I've got work to do," she replied as she returned to her computer.

I turned to Jenny as she was logging on to the computer, sat like nothing had just happened.

"You good?"

"Yeah, I'm not intimidated by him," she scoffed

"Oh I know," I smiled, "see you in the morning."

"Cool, I'll see you tomorrow."

Jenny waved as I picked up my things and walked out of the classroom to get in my car.

I'll be completely honest, obviously, I did not see this incident coming but I had been waiting for something serious and undisputable that I could report back to Liz to get rid of Darrell because he was just the worst person to have working in a school, especially with the types of students we had. So when he started screaming and shouting I did not intervene at all, I just wanted him to dig himself into a hole witnessed by everybody, including Hopeless, that would lead to his dismissal. I knew that Darrell was employed through the agency and having worked for the same agency myself I knew that he could be let go with no warnings or appeals if the management decided to do so. Clearly he should have been given the boot a long time ago but now they had an unequivocal reason that they could not hide from or gloss over. So after I left work and got in my car I drove around the corner, pulled over to the side of the road and wrote the entire incident up in an email and sent it to Liz whilst it was still fresh in my mind.

The next day I could not believe what I saw, Darrell was back in work as normal. Liz must not have got my email I naively thought. I went down to her office and asked her if she read my email and she said that she did and that she was investigating what had happened. I was stunned, I had no doubts that I was not the only one who'd emailed her, but she insisted that she was taking it seriously and that she had asked everyone who witnessed any part of the incident to write a statement. She was then going to be having one to one meetings with everyone to discuss what happened over the next two days. I thought it was a bit unnecessary but was willing to go with it for now and I left.

During my one to one meeting, I mentioned to Liz that I knew that if she wanted to get rid of Darrell she could do so immediately because he was an agency member of staff, and her response to this was strange to say the least.

"I have taken advice from HR and they have said that I cannot just let him go because he has the same rights as any other permanently employed member of staff," she said.

This was ostensibly completely false (but also kind of true because she was dodgy as fuck, but more on that later). After multiple members of staff told Liz what had happened, that Darrell was the aggressor, that they feared for Jenny's safety, that he was not safe to have around children and all of the other shit that was abundantly clear, Liz came to the conclusion that it was in her words 'Six of one and half dozen of the other'. She said both Darrell and Jenny had been in the wrong, but ultimately that it was no big deal and that he should still be working as the behaviour support manager. It was at his point that I realised just how bad the situation was and how much worse it could get at the school.

BATTLING THE CHIMAERA PART ONE

Things had gotten so bad at the PRU since Liz took charge that it was becoming dangerous, and being aided and abetted by Hopeless and Darrell things were never going to get any better. I had tried to address the issues with Liz directly but it was clear that this was futile, so I decided to try another method to restore some relative sanity and order before something seriously detrimental happened. The three of them had fused into a Chimaera-like beast composed of incompetence, insanity and carelessness, a beast that must be tamed, caged or destroyed… but how do you kill The Chimaera?

After a relatively quick discussion with Jenny and Kate, I decided to write a letter to Liz's boss explaining the situation in the hope that something would be done, between the three of us we managed to go through all of the logs we'd recorded on the school system and emails that we had sent regarding the many incidents that had occurred and collate it all. I then sent the email anonymously to her boss. Unfortunately, after two days of waiting I did not get a response back, so Maggie, after being brought up to speed about the email in a discussion with Kate, gave me the whistleblowing email address for the local council. This is a copy of the email that was sent.

To whom it may concern

We are writing this email as we have many concerns about things that have happened at ***** and feel that we are unable to trust management to deal with this issue effectively and in the appropriate manner. There have been various incidents that have happened involving a member of staff from the agency ***** named Darrell *****. All of the following issues that we will describe have been reported directly to either Liz ***** or ***** Hope and in each case, either nothing or very little has been done.

Darrell started working at ***** in November/December as a TA. During these months there were concerns about him play fighting and wrestling with students in and out of lessons, we challenged him on this issue and raised it with management, nothing was done. Later in the same month, there was an incident where Darrell after being sworn at multiple times by a student responded 'You and me, outside now.' This incident was discussed with him immediately after by a member of staff who witnessed the incident however management did nothing.

Darrell knows the family of one of our most challenging students Kingsley ***** which has created a conflict of interest and safeguarding issue. Staff suspected that this particular student was being violently treated at home, Darrell stated to a member of staff that he knows the father of this student and suggested that he could resolve the issue out of the centre through implied violence and or intimidation. On 25th January the same student told a member of staff that he and Darrell 'had a secret', eventually, he told the member of staff that he was told by Darrell that if he continues to talk about his home life with members of staff here he will be taken into care.

In February, Darrell told a member of staff that he is aware that Kingsley's father was a 'ruthless' and violent man but that he thought that he kept this lifestyle separate from his home life, however after visiting their home he was convinced that there was violence towards the child, he claimed to find the student was terrified and shaking and kept his head down the whole time. When commenting on this, Darrell stated that calling this parent evil was 'putting it nicely' but he has not logged or reported this information as far as we are aware.

On 21st March Darrell used his knowledge of Kingsley's 'ruthless' parent to intimidate him when trying to get him to go to lessons by saying to him, 'watch when I come round your house later and tell your Dad everything you've done. Watch what happens.'

In early February a staff member took a phone call from a parent who was extremely upset and in tears after her child was described to her by Darrell as a 'disgusting child' who staff have had enough of.

On 1st March two students were involved in an incident and were told to go to see Darrell in Behaviour Support. One of the students, Paul, was told by Darrell that he knew the other student's step-father and that he will come to the school and stab him. Paul, feeling threatened by what Darrell had said to him told two members of staff before being sent home. When this was brought up in the staff meeting the following day the issue was brushed under the carpet by management.

On the 3rd March, a concern was put in by a member of staff after one student was heard telling another, Darrell offered to get him an ounce of cannabis. The member of staff reported this to Liz *****, who refused to take it any further after talking to the student as he now claimed to have said the name Darren and not Darrell. The member of staff who heard the conversation is one hundred per cent certain of what they heard but the matter was left and her log of the incident appears to have been deleted from the system.

On the 9th of March, one of the students was sent home early, after going to reception to collect his belongings Darrell took his phone and refused to give it back to him. Staff witnessed Darrell intimidating and teasing the student while refusing to give him the phone and allow him to go home. The student who is known to self-harm ended up injuring himself after repeatedly punching walls in frustration and anger and pleading with the witnessing staff member to get the phone back from Darrell so that he could go home. Staff managed to get the phone back to the student and had to take him to the hospital after talking to him and calming him down. While this was going on Darrell was calling Liz ***** to give his version of events before any other members of staff could state their concerns. The following day when the issue was raised with management in the morning meeting, staff were told that the student 'should have been off-site' (which he was unable to do having not been given his property) that 'Darrell was frustrated' and that 'it's not important' and 'is being dealt with' no actual information was given despite many direct questions by staff and little to no information has been recorded. We later found out that the student, in fact, had broken bones in his hand however once again this is not logged anywhere as far as we can tell.

On the 23rd of March at the end of the school day, a major incident happened which resulted in Darrell screaming obscene and threatening verbal abuse at Jenny (a member of staff), being very aggressive and intimidating. He was held back by various members of staff and told to leave on multiple occasions but continued to try and get at her, had other members of staff not been there to prevent him from getting to her many of us feel that he would have physically assaulted her, we feared for her safety and some for their own safety also. The way that this situation has been handled so far is utterly disgraceful, Darrell was allowed to come back into work the next day alongside Jenny and various other members of staff who felt unsafe. He appears to be getting protected and coached by management on what he should do and how to avoid any more negative attention.

On the 27th of March, some members of staff were invited to talk to Liz and provide information regarding the incident involving Jenny and Darrell and how the PRU is being ran, many of us feel that this was used more as an opportunity to gather information to protect Darrell by finding out information that may be used against him in preparation for defence and/or to try to gain any information they may use against Jenny. When we questioned Liz on why Darrell was allowed back to work the day after such a serious incident she told us that she had taken advice from the HR department about the incident and that they had advised her to allow him back to work, many members of staff who have worked for ***** and other agencies find this highly doubtful and feel that we have been lied to. A representative from the HR department did come into ***** on 29th of March and spoke to Liz about the situation, however immediately after she had left the building Liz went for a private meeting with Darrell which many of us believe was to relay the details of the conversation to him.

Darrell's role at ***** started as a TA and very quickly turned into the newly created position of Behaviour Support Manager, this role was assigned to him without any other staff's knowledge and has since been advertised along with other jobs online. He has applied for the permanent position in this newly created role and despite the various issues that have been highlighted in this email staff feel that given the relationship between Liz and Darrell he will get it regardless of whether or not he is suitable. We are all aware and accept that it is not our decision to make and are not suggesting that the role should be given to an existing member of staff, however, given the various issues that have been highlighted we do feel that employing him in this capacity would not only be detrimental to the team but will inevitably cause problems for the many vulnerable children that we have a duty to protect, care for and educate.

The very fact that we feel the need to write this email to you should highlight the severity of the situation here. A large portion of the staff here feel that we now work in an unprofessional environment and many have commented that they feel that if things carry on the way that they are at the moment they will have no choice but to leave and find employment elsewhere. We are all very passionate about the work that we do and the students with whom we work.

We would like an unbiased outsider to discuss issues with staff so that we can talk openly and feel that we are being taken seriously; not only regarding Darrell but regarding any other concerns that staff have and feel have been or will be swept under the carpet. Everything that happens in this building will directly or indirectly impact the children; we would like to prevent this from happening.

Regards

***** Staff

An hour and a half after sending the email I got a response saying that the issues raised were being explored. The following day I got another email asking if I would be willing to meet with the investigative team. I was a little apprehensive at first but I understood that if something was going to be done about the current situation somebody had to raise their head above the parapet and put their name and face to the email. The team assured me that I would remain anonymous to everybody throughout the investigation unless I was required to testify in court. Jenny, Kate and Grant came with me to meet with the team as they were also willing to do the same and the investigation progressed to the next level.

After approximately three weeks of secret meetings in the pub, covert emails, a shit load of phone calls and visits to the PRU by the council's auditors, and Liz and Hopeless being called into multiple meetings at the council house where I can only assume they were relentlessly grilled judging by the state of them upon their return, things began to get very awkward at the PRU. Liz and Hopeless each lost a considerable amount of weight and were looking more and more stressed out and dishevelled by the day.

It was obvious that Liz and Hopeless assumed that Jenny had been the one to bring the barrage of investigations to their door, Jenny already had an ongoing grievance with Hopeless, and they were constantly trying to either push her out, make her look bad or were just generally horrible to her. They also targeted Grant as he was also becoming increasingly vocal about how they were running things. Kate and I managed to stay out of their firing line however we assumed it was just a matter of time before they came for us too.

After a month or so Darrell stopped coming into work, there was no explanation from management about why he wasn't in and we initially just thought he was off sick, however, when we went for another rendezvous at the pub with the auditing team and mentioned that he hadn't been at work for a while their faces told us everything we needed to know... He was gone for good. And then there were two.

NOTHING TO LOSE

Natalie used to do home visits to meet recently excluded pupils, she would find out a bit about them and report back to the rest of the staff before they arrived at the PRU for their first day. She came to tell us about a boy called Daniel, he was in year seven and was kicked out of school for persistent disruptive behaviour.

Daniel was recently placed into a care home as were his four younger sisters, due to his mother prioritising prostitution to support her heroin addiction over the safety and well-being of her children. For the simple fact that Daniel looked like his father, despite his adoration for her, his mother despised him. According to his files, she was quoted as stating during a Child In Need meeting 'I want to get all my kids back apart from him' pointing at Daniel. To hear his story was truly heartbreaking.

For the first six months of Daniel joining our school, he refused to do any work in my lessons and getting him to complete the slightest thing was like getting blood from a stone. Daniel's life experiences had clearly messed with his head, he would sit in lessons with me and randomly out of the blue ask inappropriate questions. A regular conversation with him would go as follows

"Sir, do you wanna buy some drugs?"

"No thanks Dan, why would you ask me that?"

"Just in case you wanted some drugs."

"Dan, mate, you know I have to log when you say stuff like that don't you? We've had this conversation before."

"Don't log it! I want to see my mom and I won't be able to if you log it."

"I have to log it, Dan, like I've told you before, you need to stop saying stuff like that to me."

"I fucking hate you, you're a cunt, this school's shit."

In all honesty, I absolutely hated lessons with Daniel at first, he and another boy called Matthew were the only two year-sevens at the time and my god they were the most annoying students in the school. Teaching Daniel anything was damn near impossible, not only because he was so immature but because his mental health was in free fall. After months of attempting to teach the most basic ICT lessons, I had achieved nothing. I was spending my evenings planning all sorts of engaging lessons and activities, creating resources, inventing games and nothing was working, they were just completely uninterested.

As a teacher, constantly trying your hardest to connect

with and engage your pupils, revamping and pivoting numerous times from one thing to another to teach something is depressing when it's not even given a chance by the students. Literally, everything that I tried was instantly rejected and thrown back in my face, I would put a piece of paper in front of Daniel and he would immediately rip it up and throw it across the room without even glancing at what was on it, I tried getting him to work on the computer and he would not even log in. Once, I took a computer apart to try and teach him about the hardware components inside the computer and he threw the parts around the classroom trying to break them.

After speaking to other teachers I found that everybody was on the brink of giving up on them entirely, they (Daniel in particular) were stressing everybody out and making going to work miserable.

One day I got to work and was sat at my desk looking at my timetable, just seeing their class was enough to put me in a bad mood for the entire day. I hadn't planned anything for them to do because I had literally tried everything that I could think of and was completely out of ideas, not to mention absolutely sapped of motivation. I sat for about fifteen minutes in silence, thinking about what and how I should proceed with them and reached the conclusion that they just were not ready or able to learn anything because their behaviour was just so shit, they were unteachable. I decided that I was going to have to completely scrap the idea of teaching them anything and focus solely on getting their behaviour to a place where they were actually able to function in the classroom.

My strategy was simple, refuse to teach them or set them any work at all. When they arrived at my classroom later that day, before I even let them into the room I told them the new situation.

"This is the way it is now boys, I'm done trying to teach you anything. You don't want to learn, fine. I am no longer going to even try and teach you anything."

The boys looked at me apprehensively.

"What d'ya mean?" Said Daniel.

"I mean from now on you can come to my lessons and do whatever you want, as long as it is not illegal, dangerous, clearly completely inappropriate, or something that needs to take part outside of the classroom."

"Why?" Asked Daniel

"Does it matter? You either agree, or you don't and I set you some work to do."

"Fuck that... Can we play games on the computer?"

"If you want, it's up to you."

"Yeah fuck it then I'm playing games."

The boys walked into the classroom and sat down, whilst they logged on to the computer I told them that if at any point they wanted to leave the room the only two places they were allowed to go were to the toilet or to speak to Natalie for ten minutes and then they had to come back. It was a risky strategy but I had nothing to lose.

Natalie was the behaviour support manager and at the time she was about four or five months pregnant. Daniel always wanted to talk to her about her soon to be born baby and was very protective of her, for example, if students were blocking up the corridor he would walk in front of her and clear a path for her to get where she was going. I think speaking to her about her baby was nice for him because he missed his younger siblings so much. Daniel longed to see his little sisters and would show me videos of him playing with them on his YouTube channel, I could see the pain in his eyes as he stared silently at the screen watching them all jumping on the bed and singing songs. Daniel had recently been placed into the care of a lovely woman named Alice. Daniel hated her but it was clearly because he was away from his other younger siblings who I believe were all together and living with their mother for at least a part of the week, I assume based on what we had been told previously that his mother decided that she did not want Daniel back.

As you can imagine, opting to not teach the year sevens did not sit well with management nor with the other teachers to be honest, I mean it was no secret around the school that I was not planning any work for them to do, setting any tasks or expecting anything constructive to be done in my lessons. They would walk into my classroom and I would tell them to do whatever they want, I would then try and pick moments to engage them in conversation so that I could learn more about them, they could learn more about me and hopefully build a better relationship with them.

The one person who did totally support my efforts however was Natalie, and that's who I needed the most for my endeavour. Matthew would sit and play games online every lesson but after about a month of doing nothing but play games, Daniel got bored and decided that he wanted to make superhero cards, sort of like Marvel and DC Top Trumps, which I was more than happy to help him create. After creating the cards for another month or so, I then suggested that he expanded his idea into making a board game which he loved.

Every lesson Natalie, who was now probably about seven months pregnant, would come to my classroom and start dancing at my window with her giant bump (like doing the full-on running man routine because she was completely fucking mental) and pop in to see how he was progressing with his game. Daniel would tell her about whatever new developments we had come up with, the rules we had made up, show her the board he designed, the character cards he created and everything else. It was awesome! Daniel eventually finished his game, we printed it all out, cut out the cards, made a box for it and he was extremely proud of it.

Matthew left the PRU because his parents moved house and were no longer in the area but by the end of the year, working with Daniel I slowly began implementing actual lessons again. I had him four times a week so I initially said he could have three free lessons as long as the first lesson of the week he did the work that I set him. Eventually, this was increased to two lessons a week, and finally three lessons of my work and one free lesson. During his free lessons, I would try to engage him in other activities, again trying to build up a positive relationship with him, it didn't always work but one thing that he loved to do was maintenance on my car. Over the year, every time I needed to do minor repairs on my car I would watch tutorial videos with him on YouTube and then I would take him out to the car park and guide him through the process. Together we changed my indicator, headlamp and brake light bulbs, installed a new brake light switch, topped up the oil and water, checked the air pressure on the wheels and plenty more (my car was not in the best shape so there was often something to be done), one day I even brought in some plastic overalls and he helped me wash it.

When new students joined his group in year eight I continued with the same strategy, not because the new students also needed it but because I had already established routine with Daniel and felt it was only fair to continue it. Kate was assigned as the teaching assistant to his group at this point and she and I continued to push Daniel to achieve positive learning outcomes in my lessons using this strategy.

By the time Daniel reached year nine he had been living with his foster carer Alice for a long time and was well looked after by her, he had built a positive relationship with her and she eventually adopted him and got him into a school in her local area which meant he had to leave the PRU. When he left the PRU he was a completely different boy, he had achieved so much in my lessons and across the school in general. His social skills had improved and his behaviour was positively unbelievable, obviously, this was not entirely down to me, his foster carer, Alice was an amazing woman who really did wonders for him and worked with the staff to ensure that we were all aiming towards the same goals and being consistent with rules and expectations. All of the other staff in the PRU also worked really hard to get him to the place that he was when he left. I will say this though when he left he bought me, Natalie and Kate chocolates and a beer and fuck all for anybody else, so that's got to count for something.

HE PUSHED ME LIKE HE WANTED IT

Gina and Sarah arrived to my lesson on time, so I set them their task and left them with the teaching assistant whilst I went looking for Carl. As usual, I knew exactly where to find him, I walked into the school car park stared at the roof for a few seconds and waited for the inevitable plume of smoke.

"Yo, Big Man!" I shouted.

Carl sat up with a big grin on his face.

"Yes, likkle man! Wha'gwarn?" He shouted back as he took a puff of his vape.

"What's happening, you coming down?"

"Fuck knows, just chillin' enit."

Carl took another puff of his vape

"You coming to the lesson today or what?" I shouted

"What have I got you now?"

"Yeah man, why d'ya think I'm out here, get down here quick before management see you up there and exclude you again."

Carl got down from the roof and came to the lesson. In this lesson I had a teaching assistant sent from the agency, I can't remember his name but I do remember, he had been at the school for a few days. He seemed alright to me but there was a rumour circulating around that he had made a comment about one of the girls' breasts. Apparently, one of the boys was in the corridor lying on one of the girls with his head on her chest. This girl had particularly big breasts and according to the students, the teaching assistant said to the boy 'you look like you're enjoying those lovely pillows.' Now I don't know how much truth there was behind it, but what I do know is once a rumour like that starts, it's hard to stop it from spreading like Khloe Kardashian's legs at an NBA game, especially in the PRU and especially when the students start adding their own little details on to what they were originally told. If it was given a week I guarantee the rumour would have made Jeffrey Epstein look like the Dalai Lama compared to this guy.

Anyway, so it's me, Carl and the teaching assistant in the classroom. The girls, Gina and Sarah are standing just outside the door refusing to come back in the lesson now because they too have heard this rumour about the teaching assistant's leisure time interests being shared by the likes of Michael Jackson and R. Kelly (and no I don't mean he wrote chart-topping music). I asked the teaching assistant to go and tell the girls to come to the lesson and within one minute of him being out of the classroom he was being shouted at by them and called a 'dirty fucking paedo'. Not being one to miss out on the drama Carl went to go and investigate.

I found myself in the corridor outside of my classroom with the two girls in one corner, the teaching assistant in another and Carl in another. I walked over to the girls and began talking to them to try and convince them to come to my lesson and the teaching assistant walked over to Carl, who immediately started to make paedophile jokes and puns.

"I want to go the toilet but I don't wanna miss anything. I really need to PAEDO." Carl chuckled. "Come on guys, this is all just NONCE-sense. Can't we all just be SAVILLE to each other?"

Trying not to laugh, I turned around to see the teaching assistant nose to nose with Carl and before I could open my mouth to speak Carl started swinging. A barrage of haymakers were being launched at the teaching assistant and connecting with speed, the teaching assistant was trying to block his face with one hand and catch or parry the fists hurtling towards him with the other, but Carl was firing off shots like Mike Tyson in his prime, headshots, body blows one after another bang, bang, bang, one in the chin, one in the kidney, one in the nose, one in the liver, it was carnage. I ran over to intervene and jumped in between them hoping not to catch a right hook to the jaw, I turned Carl around by the shoulders and marched him straight out of the front doors of the school and up the road. He was in a state of rage that I hadn't seen from him before and kept repeating the same thing.

"I dunno who he thinks he is, trying to take me for some fucking dickhead, I'm no fucking dickhead."

I kept my hand on his shoulder and just kept on walking with him up the road and around the corner. We stopped walking after a hundred metres or so and sat on the curb. Carl's hands were trembling as the adrenaline raced around his body.

"What the hell was that Big Man?" I asked.

Carl took a moment to gain some composure, he was breathing heavily and still trembling slightly.

"Foe, I was just popping some jokes ya get me? And the geezer full-on pushed me."

"What? He pushed you?"

"He fucking pushed me!"

"Alright listen, you need to be very clear with me here Big Man because you know this is going to be taken seriously. You just attacked a member of staff which is not like you at all..."

"I'm telling you now Foe, the fucking prick pushed me proper, and I don't care who he is if he's going on like that then he's gonna get it! It weren't even like he was trying to restrain me or move me, you know like how you or Grant might sometimes do when I'm fucking about too much. Nah fam, he pushed me. He pushed me like he wanted it. Like this." Carl then pushed me in the chest with both hands. "But he done it hard, so I like, stumbled back into the wall ya get me?"

"Alright cool, when I go back to the school I'll let them know what you said but for now we'll chill here for a bit. I don't think it's a good idea to go back just yet, you know what I mean? We'll just sit here and chill for a bit yeah?"

We sat next to each other on the curb in silence for about a minute, Carl had his head between his knees and was spitting little bits of saliva onto the floor. Carl started welling up, he looked up to the sky attempting to keep the tears from falling down his face.

"I've fucked it now you know Foe," he said solemnly

"What d'ya mean? We'll get it sorted man don't worry," I said as I placed my hand on his shoulder for reassurance.

"Nah, you don't understand, my mom and dad are gonna kick me out now. They've already said to me one more thing and that's it, they're gonna put me into care, they don't want me about anymore."

"They told you that?"

"Yeah my old man's on about he's had enough of me since I got kicked out of mainstream, he said I embarrass him." Tears started to trickle down Carl's bright red cheeks. "But he don't listen to anything I say, just tells me to get out all the time. I've been stopping on my pal's sofa for the last couple weeks 'cause he thinks I took his money, which I promise you now I never."

"Fucking hell man."

"He lost like, about a oner or summat and then said I robbed it. So I went back to the yard to get some clean clothes the other day and he'd gone through all my stuff, my room was fucked up bruv I swear. Obviously, I got pissed off enit and told him I'd smack him up. Then because I threatened to bang him after he's went through my room, he's on about I've got no respect."

"Bloody hell man, what's your mom said about all this, can't you talk to her and try to...?"

"You're mad ent ya, 'cause I said I'd bang my old man out my marj said she don't reckon it's safe for her and my little brother to have me about, like I'm gonna do summat to a ten-year-old kid or a woman, my marj as well ya get me?"

"Yeah man, of course, Jesus. That's a lot to deal with."

"I don't wanna go into care Foe, what the fuck am I gonna do then, my life will be shit fam, once you're in care your life's pretty much done, I'm blatantly gonna fail my GCSEs, then what? I'll have nothing."

Carl wiped the snot from his upper lip with his sleeve and dabbed his eyes dry with the inside of his hood.

"Look man I know it's not as easy but try not to worry about all that right now okay. I'll ring your parents and let 'em know what happened rather than management doing it and I'll make sure they get your side of the story alright?" I tilted my head forward and looked under Carl's hoodie to make eye contact. "Obviously, I can't lie to them about what happened alright? But I'll make sure they understand why it happened, yeah? And that you did walk away with me with no problems, you know what I mean? Hopefully, they'll understand." I placed my hand on the back of Carl's head. "As for your GCSEs you know I'll help you out man, so will everyone else alright? And you know what? Telling ya the truth now yeah, GCSEs aren't everything Big Man, honestly, you can still get places without them."

"Alright Foe, I appreciate that still."

Carl and I stood up, he wiped his face with his hoodie once more and we walked back towards the school.

CARL'S LAST DAY

Carl strolled up to my lesson and as always he was not wearing his school hoodie, I don't know why he hated wearing his hoodie so much especially because as far as school uniforms go, a hoodie is about as relaxed as it can get. There were no other requirements or restrictions regarding uniform other than you must wear the school hoodie and no jeans allowed, so considering that most kids go to school in a stiff shirt, a funky looking tie, trousers with a perfectly ironed crease, stiff shoes and a thick as fuck jumper or a blazer that feels about as comfortable as a straightjacket constructed from rusty baking trays, you'd think he'd be all for it, alas he was not.

"Where's your hoodie Big Man?" I enquired as I stopped him at my classroom door.

"I dunno ya know, err I think it's in Natalie's room."

I pointed in the direction of Natalie's room and gestured with my head for him to go and retrieve his hoodie. Despite the room being literally fifteen paces from my own a full five minutes passed before he returned... with no hoodie.

"What happened, I thought you went to get your hoodie?" I laughed.

"Likkle Man, I dunno where it is?" Came the slurred response.

"Did you leave it next door in art?" Gina asked, attempting to help Carl locate the elusive garment.

"I rar might have still," said Carl.

Carl went off again only to return a couple of minutes later with no hoodie. This was a daily occurrence with Carl but today I just couldn't be bothered to send him off from room to room around the school hoodie hunting, so instead I went to reception with him to see if it had been handed in or if there was a spare one which he could wear for the day to prevent him from being sent home. Fortunately, his hoodie had been put in the office so he went to the reception window at the front of the building to collect it. Maggie handed Carl the hoodie in a carrier bag.

"Here you go lovely, don't lose it this time," she smiled.

Carl took the hoodie, said thanks and turned around but rather than returning with me to the classroom he decided to go outside the front of the building to have a puff on his vape.

"Yo! What are you doing Big Man? Put that away, get your hoodie on, lesson time let's go let's go" I said holding the door open for him.

Now I would love to tell you that Carl decided he'd procrastinated enough at this point and came to engage in some valuable education, but no, instead he pretended to slip on some imaginary substance on the floor, kicking his feet out one after the other whilst windmilling his arms like a cartoon character slipping on a banana skin and released the bag containing his hoodie up over his head and onto the school roof.

"What the hell was that?!" I asked as I burst out laughing.

"I slipped," he said with a massive smile on his face.

"Slipped on what mate? There's nothing there," I howled.

"Look Likkle Man, it just slipped out my hand, don't worry I'll go get it."

"Noooo! Bloody hell man just leave it, I'll try and sort your uniform situation out later just come on we need to go to lesson."

As we went to walk back into the building we saw Darrell and Liz in the distance walking back over to the school from the park. They went for a walk over the park pretty much every day, and were always inappropriately flirtatious towards each other. We all, staff and students thought it was weird. Upon entering the classroom Carl started rambling about how he's convinced that Liz and Darrell go for little walks over the park and get stoned before they head back to Liz's office for a quickie.

"I guarantee she's just been sucking him off in the bushes." Carl declared. "I'm telling ya, they go over there build a massive blunt, blaze it up and then Darrell's like 'Yo bitch wanna taste the BBC, my jizz will get rid of your dry mouth' then they come back to her office and he smashes the back end out of her over the desk."

Now I know as a professional I should not laugh at such vulgarity, but I'm telling you now it was fucking hilarious and trying to hold in the laughter while the other students pissed themselves was no easy task. Carl then went into a full theatrical mime performance of Darrell banging Liz over the desk. He had his knees slightly bent as he's furiously gyrating his hips back and forth, his left arm outstretched clutching onto an invisible head of hair and his right hand slapping the imaginary buttocks of the headteacher alternating from forehand on the right arse cheek to a backhand on the left. He was letting out the loudest and most over-exaggerated orgasmic moans too, ones that would make the people on PornHub stop mid-scene and give him a standing ovation.

"That's why she's going bald, 'cause Darrell's pulling her hair when he's back shotting her!" He shouted.

He was being so loud at this point that half of the surrounding neighbourhood must have been able to hear him let alone the people within the school, and despite myself and the others in the room trying to get him to calm down and be quiet, all the while struggling to breathe due to the laughing fit he'd induced in all of us, it was too late he'd gone into method acting mode and was lost in the character. Now it was time for the grand finale, Carl sat down and leant back on his chair so it was at a forty-five-degree angle resting on the corner of the desk, he threw his legs straight up and out wide in the air and with his legs akimbo he started frantically rubbing his imaginary clitoris.

"Cum on my face Darrell you filthy fuck!" He screamed. "Empty them balls and drench me with your load!"

It was at this precise moment that the door flew open and a red-faced Liz stood in the doorway. Having witnessed her orgasm being acted out by a fifteen-year-old boy through the window she was both embarrassed and furious. Everybody apart from Carl went quiet immediately.

"Carl! My office!"

Startled by the interruption to his one-man show, Carl fell off of his chair accidentally kicking Gina in the face as he fell, and once again we all burst out laughing including Gina whilst clutching her forehead in pain.

Roughly ten minutes later and just before break time was due to start Carl returned and was stood outside the door waiting to be let in. As he stood waiting there I could hear Hopeless arguing with another student, she had taken the student's vape off of them because they were smoking it in a lesson and had locked it inside her office. The student was asking for the vape back so that he could smoke it outside at break time because he was trying to quit smoking cigarettes. As break was just starting all of the students had begun leaving their classes, and as they walked past the two arguing they decided to join in on the student's behalf saying that Hopeless should give the student the vape back during break time. Carl also decided to chip in, commenting in front of everyone.

"If she locked my vape in her office, I'd just press the fire alarm to unlock the door and then walk in and get it."

This was because all of the doors used a magnetic locking system that automatically turned off once the fire alarm was triggered, unlocking every door in the building. Unsurprisingly, a couple of minutes into break time the fire alarm went off. A few students were running in and out of classrooms and offices that they shouldn't be in attempting to cause havoc however the majority of the students were already outside smoking as was the norm, one of the students included in this bunch was Carl. Despite being seen stood outside near two members of staff when the alarm went off Liz and Hopeless immediately marched over to Carl and told him he was being excluded for setting off the fire alarm. Understandably Carl was livid.

"Fuck off! I haven't even done anything I've been stood here the whole time!" Carl exclaimed.

"I don't want to hear it, you're going home," Hopeless replied, "I'm not arguing with you because I heard you say you were going to do it earlier."

"What are you talking about you dumb bitch, I said I WOULD have if it were mine, but obviously it wasn't mine was it so why would I care?!" He shouted.

Gina and a few other students who were around all started to corroborate Carl's defence but Liz and Hopeless were having none of it.

"I don't wanna hear it!" Hopeless yelled as she walked away.

While this was going on, I and the rest of the staff were attempting to get all of the students to the fire meeting point, I walked over to Carl and the other students who were still arguing with Liz. Carl turned to me looking extremely pissed off and upset.

"Foe, will you tell her I've been stood here the whole time when the fire alarm went off?"

"Yeah, he was here I could see him from where I was stood, it can't have been him." I explained.

"Well, you're always setting off the fire alarm Carl so I'm not going to believe you am I?"

Natalie overheard what was going on and came over to us, she began explaining to Liz that she too had seen Carl stood outside smoking with his friends when the alarm went off and that he was therefore innocent. As she was explaining what she had witnessed Hopeless returned.

"Your parents have been called. You're going home," she said angrily.

"Go and get your stuff," added Liz.

Liz and Hopeless turned and walked away and Carl started shouting a load of abuse at the two of them as they strolled back into the building. Natalie and I walked slowly with Carl to the front of the building for him to collect his belongings and tried to calm him down.

"Listen, Carl, I know you didn't do it but there's nothing I can do right now, ok? I will be bringing it up again at the staff meeting tonight but for now, you're just going to have to go home." Natalie said softly.

"I know I do sometimes press the alarm Natalie but I swear on my life it weren't me. They just don't like me 'cause I take the piss out of 'em," he replied.

I could see the upset and annoyance on his face as I put my hand on his shoulder.

"Listen, Big Man, we both know it wasn't you and you heard us say to them just now that we know one hundred per cent that it couldn't have been you. But they're not listening to us, it's not fair at all but trust me I'm not going to let it go." Carl went quiet, "I know sometimes you get into trouble but you're a good kid and just know that there are people who work here like me, like Natalie, like Kate, Grant, Jen, you know. We stick up for you and fight your corner on crap like this. Sometimes though the result isn't perfect."

"He's right Carl, we do try and back you up all the time but if management say you've got to go we can only do so much" Natalie added.

"We will say something though won't we Natalie? We'll do what we can to get you back in on Monday. I'll even call your house later and let your parents know the truth, yeah?"

Carl took his belongings from the reception desk and walked off up the road.

"Monday Big Man, yeah? See you Monday" I shouted.

The following day I was sat in my living room watching TV with my fiancé when I got a phone call from Kate.

"What's up Kate?"

"Are you at home?"

"Yeah why, what's up?"

"Are you sitting down?"

I could hear her voice beginning to crack as she became more and more upset.

"What the fuck's going on Kate?"

I knew whatever she was about to say was going to be bad and in the brief pause before she uttered the following sentence I tried to prepare myself.

"Carl's dead, he hung himself last night."

And with those words my heart broke, my body was dragged to the floor in a ball and I burst into tears.

BATTLING THE CHIMAERA PART TWO

We'd gotten rid of Darrell but that was the easy part. The trouble with cutting the smallest head off of The Chimaera when its back is turned, is that its two bigger and more powerful heads are now on high alert and ready to fight back. This makes the beast far more difficult to vanquish.

Carl taking his own life was exactly the sort of thing that I and others were trying to prevent from happening when writing the email, obviously, none of us saw this specific outcome coming but we all knew something terrible was going to happen sooner or later given the circumstances. Now I'm not suggesting that the things going on at the school with management and Darrell were the only factors in Carl's suicide, Carl had mental health issues, problems at home, issues with his girlfriend and God knows what else going on, however after speaking to Ben at his funeral, one of his close friends and a former student of the

PRU, there is absolutely no doubt in my mind that these mother fuckers knowingly contributed.

Ben and I were talking about the last time we saw Carl, he told me that the last time he had seen him, Carl was pissed off and ranting about how he'd been excluded from school for having some weed on him. Carl told him that he was given the weed by Darrel to sample, only to have Darrel snitch on him to Liz when he took it with him to school the next day. According to Ben, Carl often felt bullied by management at the PRU. He said that Carl told him about multiple occasions where he would be pulled into the office with Liz and either one of her sidekicks and pressured into making written statements alleging that Grant and Jenny had taken him to the pub and other similar inappropriate activities. He also told me that they regularly threatened to inform his parents of the slightest slip up that he would make as they knew his parents were considering putting him into care. Now I can't say for certain if Carl did write or sign any kind of statement under duress, however, I do know that a few months before Carl killed himself Grant and Jenny were placed on administrative leave and this was something that really bothered him.

After Carl died the investigations really ramped up at the PRU, pretty much every other day Maggie would be telling Kate and me about another person from the local authority who called and wanted to either speak or meet with Liz or Hopeless. There were constantly people coming to the PRU unannounced and looking through all sorts of documentation and files on the computers.

After months of investigating Liz was also placed on administrative leave. Due to the crossover and impact that her investigation had on Jenny's, Jenny and her representatives were privy to a vast amount of information regarding the findings and outcomes of Liz's investigation.

Remember before when I told you Liz was dodgy as fuck, well during these investigations it was discovered that she had been committing fraud. She was paying Darrell twice for the same job, she had him on a temporary contract with the council (hence the reason the lady from HR said he had the same rights as any other employee) but she was also hiring him through the agency at the same time and therefore paying him double. If she was willing to do that, I assume that she had some way of skimming a little off of the top for herself too although this is purely speculation on my part, who knows? Maybe Carl was right and really she just wanted Darrell's dick so badly that she was willing to pay him for it.

So you might be wondering what happened to Liz. Well, Liz is now in prison where she belongs... Oh no, wait, no she isn't. This fucking cunt managed to wriggle her way out of the shit she'd caused because she hired an expensive lawyer, and the council (I assume) either didn't want to spend the money on a lengthy court case or did not want the story to be on the front page of the local or national newspapers. Instead, she was given her old job back in another department of the council, which wait for it... is in a managerial position dealing with vulnerable looked after children in care homes.

Hopeless managed to keep her job as second in command

simply because she was able to act the fool and plead ignorance to all of the shit that went on. She did try to find other jobs and went for several interviews, but unsurprisingly nobody wanted to hire her. I think the whole experience for her was like an episode of scared straight. Metaphorically speaking, she strolled into the prison thinking she was a gangster, narrowly avoided being gang-raped and beaten to a pulp and quickly decided to shut the fuck up and just do her time.

GET IN THE TAXI
YOU BITCH

At 08:30am during the staff meeting I was told that a new girl was starting and her name was Gina. I was given no background information about her from her previous school and her pupil profile was not on the system, all I knew was that she was in year nine and that she had very low attendance at her previous school. At 08:55 she was brought to my classroom for her first lesson. She was dressed like she was going on a night out, in a nice blouse, skinny jeans, and fancy looking high heeled boots. Her pink nail extensions and matching pink hair extensions were freshly done, she had long false eyelashes, was plastered in fake tan and her makeup was meticulously applied.

As she came into the classroom I introduced myself as usual but she refused point-blank to engage in any conversation with me, she wouldn't even sit down. Gina slowly walked up and down my classroom picking up items off of the desks and then either dropping them on the floor, or putting them back where they were but not in the way that they were to begin with. I ignored her behaviour at first and continued with my usual getting to know you chit chat.

"So what school did you go to before you came here...do you know any of the students here already?"

To every question I asked she said nothing, she just stared at me like I was speaking to her in Dothraki. I decided I'd leave her to settle in for a bit and told her to have a seat whenever she was ready so that we could get started. There was nobody else in the classroom so I sat in my chair at the back of the room and left her to wander around messing up my classroom. After a minute or two of silence, it was clear that she was waiting for some kind of response and therefore began to escalate the destruction, she began tearing displays off of my walls and throwing things across the room.

"Why are you tearing down my displays, Gina?" I asked calmly, "If you don't want to sit down or do any work I'm not going to force you to, but don't start destroying things in here please."

Gina then took the pot of felt pens off of my desk and threw one of them in my direction, she clearly missed on purpose but with each throw, it was obvious that she was trying to get them as close to me as possible so that I would flinch or react in some way. After about five throws with no response or flinching on my part she then began throwing them at me, the first hit me in the chest.

"Gina, please don't do that," I said.

She threw another, this time a little harder.

"Seriously Gina, you need to stop that."

She took a few steps forward so that she was about two metres away from me and looked at me with squinted eyes.

"Or what?!" She said with animosity.

Gina then took another felt pen from the pot and drew her arm back, just as she went to throw it I took a step towards her and took hold of both of her forearms.

"Get off of me, you can't touch me!" She shouted as she tried to free her arms.

"Drop the pens and I will let you go," I said sternly.

Gina started to really struggle and fought hard to over-power me, she started to push forward but was unable to and while she did this I rotated her left arm emptying the pot of felts on the floor. I could see a look of helplessness and fear come over her face as she screamed in my face.

"Get the fuck off me, you black bastard!"

Seeing that she was on the brink of tears, I let her go and quickly snatched the empty pen pot from her hand, Gina immediately turned around and stormed out of the room.

"I hate you, you're a black cunt! You're not allowed to grab me you black cunt!" She shouted as she left.

After this initial interaction, Gina left and I did not see her again for approximately six months, she did not attend school and returned part way through year ten. When I heard that she was returning to school I read all of her files (as we'd finally received them). In them it detailed that she had a very troubled family life and that she had potentially been a victim of child sexual exploitation by a group of men who groomed girls and sexually abused them at a social club in the city centre, due to this she was very distrusting of men in particular.

The next time Gina came to one of my lessons, she came in and sat down, she didn't say anything or do anything just sat there.

"Hi Gina," I said with a smile.

"I'm not doing any of your work," came the response.

"Work? Who said anything about work? Listen, obviously you don't know me yet but go and ask any of the students about me, I'm not here to make you work. If you don't want to do anything, what can I do about it really?"

Gina looked at me very confused as I waited for an answer.

"Think about it, seriously what can I do? Nothing. Obviously, if you want to do some work I've got stuff for you to do, but one thing you'll eventually learn about me is that I don't force anybody to do their work. You decide when and if you want to do work in my class."

I then sat at my desk and put on some epic fail videos on YouTube.

By the time Gina reached year eleven she was my most

promising student, she was achieving good grades and had made really good friends with her new classmates Sarah and Carl. At the end of every lesson, we would spend the last ten minutes watching videos on YouTube and on occasions when she or the others really weren't in the frame of mind to focus on work we'd do it for the entire lesson. We'd find the funniest, strangest or most amazing things we could and chat about them for the entire hour. One YouTube channel in particular that she told me about that always sticks out in my head was called Robert Helpmann which has ten videos all about somebody called Daisy. I say some BODY because all of the videos depict a dead body wrapped in bin liners with some creepy music in the background... I don't think it's real but it's definitely fucking weird.

On Thursdays, the rest of Gina's class went to do some P.E. activities off-site with an alternative provision that the PRU had links to, but Gina always refused to do it. By this point Gina and I got on extremely well, so instead of P.E. she would opt to sit in with me and we would chat about any and everything that she wanted to. Usually, she would tell me about the latest problems she was having with her controlling, mentally and emotionally abusive boyfriend. He would regularly call her whilst at school and then shout at her because he could hear boys in the background (as if she was out partying on an eighteen to thirty holiday and not clearly at school, where the majority of the students were boys). I would do my best to give her some relationship advice and build her confidence up so she would eventually have to strength and courage to leave him.

Gina and I also discussed the turbulent relationship that she had with her alcoholic father, who for Christmas gave her twenty pounds out of the sixty pounds that he got by selling her iPad. He used the other forty pounds to buy cigarettes and alcohol for himself which he consumed swiftly before passing out, Gina then had to go to the corner shop and buy a frozen pizza and a pot noodle for her Christmas dinner, which she ate alone in her bedroom.

I discussed and helped to find support for her regarding her self-harming as she used to cut her arms and thighs when things got overwhelming (part of the reason she did not want to do P.E). I would also try to help her with issues she had at work as partway through the year she'd managed to get a weekend job at a local coffee shop, the issue was that her manager was constantly trying to take advantage of her lack of knowledge regarding employment laws.

Gina also taught me many things in our Thursday sessions that I will never forget, such as how to apply fake nails, the best places to buy jewellery for my fiancé, and most memorably she taught me what a slag line is. For those who don't know, a slag line is a line that is seen usually under or around a girl's chin when they have put foundation on their face but they did not continue to apply it to their neck. It leaves a distinct line where their skin tone changes colour from that of the makeup to their actual skin colour.

The last time I saw Gina was on the day of her ICT exam, it was her final school exam and I was invigilating. Before the exam started, Gina mentioned that she was supposed to start a shift at the coffee shop at twelve as she now also worked some extra shifts during the week, she was planning to leave the exam early otherwise she'd be late. During the exam however, she was so focused on her questions that she lost track of time and didn't realise that she'd stayed longer than she intended to. When the exam finished and she realised what time it was, she asked me for a favour.

"Can you drop me round the corner to work Foe? I'm gonna be late, I lost track of time."

"Sorry I can't G, don't worry though, I noticed you were in the zone during the exam and weren't going to be on time for work, so I got Maggie to order you a taxi with the petty cash money, it should be here soon."

Gina, Sarah and I stood outside waiting for the taxi to arrive and for Sarah's mom to pick her up. Sarah's mom soon arrived and Gina and I continued talking. We talked about what she was planning on doing now that she'd left school and how she felt about leaving, she seemed a little nervous about losing the support provided by the school but was optimistic about her future, which was nice to hear. There was a moment of silence as we stood staring up the road waiting for the taxi to appear from around the corner.

"Do you remember my first-day Foe? In your lesson, d'ya remember?" She said cautiously.

"Yeah I remember."

"I was a right fucking bitch then weren't I?"

I smirked but said nothing as memories of Gina trashing my classroom and throwing pens at me raced through my mind,

Gina then turned to face me.

"I said some fucking horrible shit to you that day, remember? It was bang out of order. You know, for time now I've thought about that every Thursday when we've had them one to one lessons and I feel like a right cunt for what I said. You're one of the soundest teachers I've ever had. I suppose I always just think like... I wonder if you remember that and if you still think I'm a bit of a bitch sometimes, you know?"

Just then the taxi came around the corner.

"What do you think?" I said smiling.

Gina turned away slightly and shrugged, she stepped forward to the edge of the curb and held her arm out to signal the taxi.

"Honestly G, I'd forgiven you the second you walked back in my classroom and sat down. We all have bad days but it doesn't mean that you're a bitch for the rest of your life. Alright?"

"Thanks, Foe."

"No worries... Now get in the taxi you bitch or you're gonna be late for work."

Gina laughed and got in the taxi, we waved at each other as the taxi drove off and that was the last I saw of her.

HAVE YOU BEEN INJURED AT WORK?

Working in a PRU has risks that as a member of staff you must recognise, accept and attempt to mitigate. Some students can be very volatile and have anger management issues that take over their ability to think and act rationally, others lack common sense and never consider potential harm they could cause due to idiotic impulsivity, others are just emotionally and mentally damaged to the point where they lack any care, compassion or consideration for other people. These are the three main things that in my experience lead to the most serious staff injuries. Now it should go without saying that these are not stand-alone reasons for the injuries I'm about to describe, they are always tethered to a shit load of additional factors, however, these are as far as I'm concerned the most dominant and therefore noteworthy.

During my time as a teacher, I have known many members

of staff who have been hospitalised, leaving work with cuts, bruises, burns, sprains, fractures and an entire list of other injuries. There are far too many to mention them all and also I was not there to witness some of the most severe ones that I know of, so I will briefly mention some of the more serious injuries that have taken place based on what I was told by the injured person, other staff who did witness it and what I read about each incident on the reporting system.

Injury number one - A year ten boy called Adam arrived and was being refused entry to the school because he was not wearing the correct school uniform, he was stood in reception arguing with Super Teacher for a few minutes when Tasha, a year eleven girl who had already been let through the door and was supposed to be heading to her lesson decided to get involved. Tasha was stood on one side of the double doors, Adam was on the other side and Super Teacher was stood between them in the doorway with the door slightly open, just enough to slide half of her body through so that she could talk to Adam without him pushing passed her. After the two students had provided a sufficient amount of verbal abuse to Super Teacher (who I assume responded with her usual smugness and patronising condescension, whilst spouting dismissive orders to easily triggered teenagers... because they love that...), Tasha reached over Super Teacher through the gap in the doorway, grabbed onto Adam and began trying to pull him through the door.

Now to put it politely this girl's somatotype was undoubtedly endomorphic, to put it not so politely she was a fucking beefcake; around six feet tall and at least sixteen stone. As she attempted to drag Adam through the blocked doorway she started to yank the door to get more leverage and pull Adam through the double doors, however, with this action she was also crushing Super Teacher's arm between the two doors. Super Teacher began to scream and shout in pain but the students were in too much of a frenzy to even take any notice of her cries until there was an audible crunch and Super Teacher screamed like somebody had just pierced her eyeball with a hot knife. Tasha stopped briefly and Super Teacher began to cry and ran down the corridor clinging onto her forearm.

Coincidentally, on this day a police officer was at the school having a meeting with Carter, the headteacher, about another student. News about what had just gone on soon reached him and he left the meeting to investigate. As he walked around the corner to the reception area where Tasha was stood, he told her to sit in the reception area while things got sorted out. Tasha chose her words very carefully when she spoke to him as he was a police officer in full uniform.

"Fuck off you dickhead, I ent going anywhere. Make me!"

The police officer then took a step towards Tasha and took hold of her arm, the second he touched her she absolutely lost it and began fighting with him. By this point, there were multiple members of staff around who managed to help restrain her and get her out of the building. Super Teacher was later taken to hospital where they confirmed that her arm was indeed broken.

Injury number two - Marcus was in a rage because he was not able to cook what he wanted to in his food lesson, Sue had asked him what he wanted to cook in his previous lesson so that she could buy the ingredients for him (which she did) but on the day that he was supposed to cook it, he changed his mind and wanted to cook something else. Obviously, the ingredients he initially requested were available and so he could have still cooked whatever that particular meal was and waited until the following week to cook this new thing, but instead, this was enough to send him into the sort of crazed tantrum that you would only expect to see from a crack-addicted toddler.

As the thirteen-year-old boy stormed out of the room screaming a barrage of abuse at Sue, she ran to the door attempting to keep him calm and in the lesson. Sue was stood in the doorway with her hand on the door frame when Marcus kicked the door as hard as he could, this caused the door to slam shut on Sue's fingers amputating the top of her middle finger in the process. Sue screamed until she had no air left in her lungs as blood pissed out of her hand like a deleted scene from the movie Saw, the top of her finger hung on by a thin strand of skin and Marcus stormed off whilst continuing to give her a mouthful of verbal abuse.

Marcus then went home and wrote a message on social media laughing about the injury he'd caused and saying he doesn't care if she's hurt because she's a bitch for not allowing him to make the food that he wanted, literally adding insult to injury. Marcus was initially excluded for five days, and Sue was obviously not at work for a long, long time. During the five days that Marcus was excluded, almost all of the students decided they needed to avenge Sue and made it crystal clear to staff that the next time they saw Marcus they were going to jump him and beat him to death. For his own safety, Marcus was never allowed to return to the school.

Injury number three - The magnetic lock on the science room door was weak for some reason and all of the students knew it. This meant that they could run up to it and boot it open with ease. They used to do this relatively regularly just to cause havoc in the science room because the science teacher at the time was fucking useless, they knew that regardless of which class was in there the students would be up for causing mayhem because there was absolutely zero possibility that any teaching or learning was taking place in there.

One day, Carl ran down to the science room and kicked the door open as usual, however he did not know that Kate was sat on the other side of it. The door smashed straight into the side of Kate's head knocking her completely off of her chair. For weeks after this Kate complained of headaches and eventually was sent for a CT scan where they discovered that the blow from the door had caused a brain aneurysm.

Injury number four - The art teacher was a guy called Patrick, he was about sixty years old, he was a bit posh but was generally a nice guy. He used to get annoyed that the students would break or waste equipment and resources in his classroom and decided that he was going to try and teach the students to appreciate the things that they have. His idea was simple, if a student breaks a piece of equipment, he would make a note of it and then in subsequent lessons give them the same broken equipment to work with rather than giving them a brand new item to break.

One-day Dean broke a pencil into multiple small pieces during the lesson, for no reason whatsoever other than he just felt like it. In the following lesson when Dean arrived and asked for a 2B, Patrick gave him the exact same broken bits of pencil and a pencil sharpener, he told Dean that because he had broken the pencil he now had to use the broken pencil to continue his drawing. Dean was not impressed by Patrick's efforts to recycle and reuse damaged equipment, so he stood up from his chair and shouted at Patrick.

"Are you a fucking mong or something? Give us a proper fucking pencil now!"

Patrick, stuck to his guns and refused to give Dean a new pencil and Dean proceeded to punch Patrick full force in the face smashing his glasses, knocking him halfway across the room and skidding across the tiled floor. Patrick was taken to the hospital with a concussion and did not return to the PRU ever again.

I CAN'T DEAL WITH THIS SHIT

The pupils were already in a heightened state of hyperactivity and as I had no lessons for periods one and two, I had the pleasure of being on behaviour management duty all morning. This pretty much consisted of me haranguing children back into their retrospective lessons when they decided (as they frequently did) to walk out of a class because they couldn't be arsed to do any work, found it too difficult, too boring or whatever else they came up with as an excuse.

I had just managed to clear the corridor of students and was enjoying my moment of bliss when all of a sudden the maths teacher, Annika, barged past me in a frenzied state. She was sort of frog-marching at arm's length a very sheepish pupil down the corridor. He was a year eight boy named George. George was short and very fat, he had blonde curtains like he was fresh out of the nineties and often whined like a four-year-old if he did not get his own way. His voice hadn't broken yet which exacerbated the extremely irritating whining and made you feel like you were dealing with a primary school child whenever you had to address his behaviour. The other students also hated George for similar reasons, they found him annoying and therefore he was a loner. So when I saw him been escorted hastily down the hallway I assumed that he had done something to piss Annika off, that or he was being removed for his own safety before one of the other students shivved him in the face with a compass.

As I watched the situation unfold I was somewhat perplexed, normally George would be creating a scene when being directed to do something, but he was being rather compliant.

"Is everything okay Annika?" I probed as I followed them down the corridor.

"No!" She said abruptly, "he needs to go to the toilet quickly!"

She then whispered something in my ear which I would only expect to hear said about an eighteen-year-old in a university rugby club on a piss up in Faliraki.

"He has taken a shit in the sink in the maths room."

My mind raced, I must have misheard her...surely. I took a moment to contemplate what was just disclosed before the reality of the situation hit me, like the acrid stench offending my nostrils.

Suddenly a stampede of pupils came spilling out of the

maths classroom gasping for fresh air as if someone had turned the air supply off, retching so hard that their bodies convulsed in pain. The teaching assistants were trying to evacuate the victims like first responders after a terrorist attack, but very rapidly they too were overwhelmed by the chemical weapon unleashed by this putrid little fucker.

I had no idea where to look or what to do. As I walked to the classroom door and looked inside the room I found my poor colleague frantically washing away the remaining smudges of shit from the sink whilst another colleague was vomiting uncontrollably on the floor like Regan MacNeil in The Exorcist.

Whilst this was happening the sink shitting sicko, began to explain himself to Annika. His justification was that he had in fact not done a shit in the sink and instead his fat naked arse cheeks had acted as a kind of plunger, dislodging some residue from the u-bend. Hence the smell.

Now whether this was the case or not, I have no idea, however, there were still remaining questions to be asked! Why the fuck did he have his arse out in the middle of a lesson in the first place? And what, for the love of God, was he doing sitting, arse plunging and/or shitting in a sink?

YOU CAN'T DRINK THAT IN HERE

One of the teaching assistants at the PRU was a woman in her fifties called Pam. By far the easiest way to describe what she looked like is to picture (or Google a picture of) Dr John Cooper Clarke. Now imagine him with white hair and thirty per cent fewer teeth.

Pam had worked at the alternative provision as a mentor for a few years before it merged with the PRU, when the two merged her role was removed and she was given a role as a teaching assistant. Pam was very outspoken which regularly caused her to fall out with other staff, in particular the teachers. In my opinion, this was mainly because she just could not adapt to the idea that she was not in charge of her own sessions anymore and that she had to take direction from the teachers.

Pam got on well with one or two of the students but many of them also disliked her for three reasons; one, she was not particularly intelligent and therefore was not very helpful to them during lessons, two, she never seemed to realise when whatever she was doing or saying was becoming annoying which pissed the students off, and three, to be honest, they also judged her based on her appearance which they often referred to as looking like a 'nitty', which a quick search on urbandictionary.com will tell you, means 'someone who overuses drugs'.

I did find Pam to be annoying but I had never really had any problems with her until this day, it was the first lesson and she turned up ten minutes late with a cup of coffee in her hand. Teaching in a computer room logically meant I did not allow drinks in the classroom, not from students or from the staff, including myself. This was for two simple reasons, one being the most obvious, if anybody spills liquid on the computers they will cause a lot of damage. And two, if the students see me or another member of staff breaking this rule they would do so too and argue this rule for an eternity.

As she walked in sipping her coffee which was full to the brim and already spilling with each step that she took, I said to her the same thing that I had said to many other teaching assistants who had walked in with a hot drink.

"I'm sorry Pam but you can't drink that in here because of the computers," while pointing at the big 'No food or drink' sign at the front of the room.

"What do you mean? I'm a member staff," she questioned with confusion.

One of the students in the class then said to her, "So what, I weren't allowed to bring my drink in and mine had a lid on."

Pam ignored both of us and continued walking towards the desk and sat down.

"Pam, what are you doing?" I said with a politely forced smile, "you can't drink that in here."

Pam gave me a 'who do you think you are' look and stood back up swiftly before devolving into a toddler-like tantrum.

"Are you serious! I have a coffee every morning, every morning I have a coffee and your telling me I can't."

She then stormed out of the classroom and slammed the door behind her. In all honesty, it was kind of funny and both the students and I did laugh a bit as she left, having said that I still thought it was ridiculous and annoying that she not only turned up late but arrived with a cup of coffee which she was already spilling on the carpet, to top it all off she did not return to the lesson.

A couple of days later I was sat in the staff room chatting with some colleagues at lunchtime and Pam walked in with a student. Now the staff room is called the staff room for a reason, it's self-explanatory and leaves no room for ambiguity, obviously, it is supposed to be for staff, and only staff. The staff room is generally considered a safe space to vent, rant and generally talk huge amounts of shit to other staff about the students that have pissed you off throughout the day, it's cathartic to get it out of your system before the next lesson. As you can imagine this is not as easy to do when a student is in the room, the room went silent almost immediately. As she walked in, I was sat with my back to the door, so I did not realise she was with a student until everybody began to shush me and tell the student to exit the staff room. The student stepped outside of the door and I continued with my usual expletive saturated rambling rant about the frustrations I'd been caused by the students, however once again the staff began to shush me and subtly point at the door. I turned to look and see the problem that they were alerting me to, Pam was stood with the door open chatting to the student.

I called over to her to get her attention and sort of half whispered, half mouthed to her.

"Close the door."

Pam once again gave me that look, then shouted at me clenching her shaking fists.

"YOU ARE SO RUDE!"

She then, once again slammed the door and stormed off huffing and puffing, leaving everybody in the staffroom very confused about what they had just witnessed. Despite the irony of her calling me rude whilst herself being rude, even though I had been quite polite, I thought I'd let it go for now and go and speak to her about it at the end of the day.

At the end of the day once the students had left, I went to go speak to her and found her in one of the meeting rooms with Lynn. I didn't really know Lynn that well, she had formerly been the assistant manager of the alternative provision before the merger but I'd heard good things about her and the limited interactions we had were positive. I popped my head in the door and asked Pam if she had a few minutes to chat, she said that she didn't and that she was busy in a meeting so I thought nothing of it and told her to come and find me when she had a minute or else I'd chat to her in the morning.

The next morning before school had started I saw her outside smoking a cigarette.

"Hi Pam," I said as I walked over to her, "I just thought I'd have a quick chat to you about yesterday since I didn't get a chance to after school, have you got five minutes?"

"No I'm busy." I was promptly told.

I looked around thinking to myself, busy with what? She was literally stood on the corner, on her own smoking and doing absolutely nothing else. Unless she was secretly also a daytime hooker I failed to see how she was currently busy but I thought there was no point in continuing to push this conversation so I left her alone.

For the rest of the week, I noticed that every time she was timetabled to be in one of my lessons she swapped with another teaching assistant or just did not turn up. In all honesty, I preferred not having her in my lessons but I thought in the interest of professionalism I'd better mention it to Carter, the headteacher. Carter suggested that I give her a day or two to cool off, then if she still refused to speak to me or come to my lessons he would set up a meeting with the three of us to discuss what was going on.

A couple of days passed and of course, Pam was still acting as salty as the dead sea and refusing to talk to me, so we were called to a meeting during our lunch break. I arrived first to

Carter's office and a minute later Pam turned up with Lynn. They both sat down and whilst doing so Pam started yapping away.

"I've brought Lynn with me as a representative and witness to this meeting, if that's not ok then I don't want to do this and I'm leaving."

Lynn had an A4 notepad opened on her lap, a pen in hand and a very serious look on her face. Pam sat next to her with the body language of a teenager who was being told off by the head-teacher as opposed to being a full-grown fucking woman. Carter agreed to Lynn sitting in with us, as did I, I just simply did not give a shit at this point and the meeting began.

Carter started, "I have brought you both here in an attempt to resolve some kind of issue that's going on between the two of you, Marvin spoke to me about it last week..."

I could not be bothered to sit and waste my lunch break in a long conversation so I quickly interjected.

"Ok Pam here's the situation, the fact that we're all sat here now is ridiculous, you're clearly still in a mood with me because I told you that you were not allowed to drink your coffee in my classroom..."

"I have a coffee every morning and nobody else minds so what makes you think you can tell me I can't. I shouldn't be getting told off by someone younger than my son."

Me being younger than your son sounds like a 'you problem', I thought to myself. I always knew that being given instructions by considerably younger people bothered her, other staff had the same issue with her but I decided to ignore that part of the comment and address the coffee situation.

"Pam, go and ask any of the other TAs and they will tell you that I say exactly the same thing to them. The room's full of computers so having drinks in the classroom is not happening. Also, I can't be arsed with the arguments from students if I allow staff to bring in drinks but not them, we all know what these kids are like and they will just see it as unfair."

Lynn and Carter nodded in agreement, while Pam jostled in her seat and avoided eye contact with me.

"Well I just found it annoying and rude that's all," she said while looking at the wall.

"Well fair enough, but I found it annoying and rude that you turned up late to my lesson with a coffee when everyone else manages to make and drink their hot drinks in the staff room every morning and get to their lessons on time, and then completely ignore me when I asked you not to bring it into my classroom. Which leads me nicely onto the incident in the staff room the other day, I was simply highlighting to you that you should not be bringing students into the staff room and that keeping the door open while you spoke to him once he was outside meant that we could not continue our private conversation. I came to try and talk to you after school because you had clearly taken it the wrong way, Lynn you were there. I said come and find me when you were done and you didn't."

Lynn nodded her head in acknowledgement as Pam continued to stare at the wall like a disgruntled child.

"The next morning I tried to speak to you again, and again you refused to talk to me. You have not turned up to any of my lessons since, which if I'm completely honest I don't really give a shit about, but at the end of the day it disrupts everybody else in the building when staff are planning lessons etcetera if you are swapping with other TAs or just not arriving at lessons."

Pam didn't say a word, she remained sitting in the chair staring at the wall. I could not believe I was talking to a woman in her fifties and not a stroppy teenager. The three of us all sat in silence looking at each other and then at Pam waiting for some kind of response. After about five seconds I looked at Carter and shrugged my shoulders.

"Pam, is there anything you'd like to say?" Asked Carter.

Pam turned to Carter looking like she was about to cry and said in the saddest and most gentile tone she could muster.

"I just don't feel comfortable and safe with him in a room, that's why I didn't want to speak to him or go to his lessons or come to this meeting on my own."

Fucking hell, I thought to myself. She doesn't feel safe? What does she think I'm going to do to her? Throw her hot coffee in her fucking face, scolding her and scarring her for the rest of her fucking life, just to teach her a fucking lesson about the importance of fucking punctuality and not fucking turning up to my fucking lesson with a hot fucking drink?! I mean yes, I'd be tempted to if I'm honest, but I probably wouldn't have.

THE PAEDO AND
THE RADICAL

Zabir was in year nine when he first joined the PRU, he was an average-sized boy with a skin fade and mini moustache, he wasn't the loudest kid in the world but was always willing to engage in conversation and he was very polite and respectful. So I was very surprised to read his file and see that he was excluded from his previous mainstream school for kicking six shades of shit out a boy and hospitalizing him. When I asked Zabir about why he felt the need to demolish the boy so badly he told me it was because the boy had called him a 'dirty fucking paki' and called his mom 'a letterbox'. Zabir's mother was from Afghanistan and his father was from Pakistan, and at the time he constituted the entire Asian, and Muslim population of the school.

Zabir was always very chilled out in lessons, his goal was to fly below the radar, meet the minimum requirements to pass qualifications and leave, he was relatively calm, very quick-witted and got on well with others. The only time I witnessed any aggression from him was when another student called him a 'fucking paki' during a game of football at lunchtime and not being one to break a trend he fucked that kid up pretty good too. Zabir was very intelligent but just could never be bothered to put any effort into any work that didn't really interest him. Any time he was given a task he would bang it out as fast as possible, doing the bare minimum to achieve a pass and then he'd strike up a conversation, we'd chat mostly about movies and recommend TV shows to each other to binge-watch on Netflix.

One day we were talking about a music video that one of the other students was in, it was one of those drill music videos where a bunch of teenagers stick their fingers up at the camera, smoke weed and pop wheelies on stolen motorbikes.

"Foe, have you seen the music video with Dion in it?" He asked.

"I haven't no, is it any good?"

"It's alright, you probably wouldn't like the music but the video is jokes," he chuckled.

"Why what's Dion doing in the video, rapping?" I enquired.

"Nah, he's just like, he chilling on the wall with his boys enit, then he does this to the camera," he said as he waved gun fingers at me.

"Oh yeah, Dion the bad man gangster then is it?" I smirked, "I'll have to check it out later... Now you, get back to your work."

"Nah let me put it on please, it's jokes."

"Just tell me what it's called and I'll check it out later."

"I'll just show you now because you won't know it's him otherwise, he's wearing his t-shirt as a bally." He persisted.

I was intrigued, I didn't know you could turn a t-shirt into a balaclava. So not being one to miss a learning opportunity I asked him to explain to me how it was done. Zabir tried to explain it to me but either he was doing a shit job or I was too dumb to get it. Whatever the case may be I was not following what he was saying. Now Zabir, demonstrating his outstanding Ofsted inspection level teaching skills recognised that a bit of differentiation was required, and to cater to my kinesthetic learning style he decided to demonstrate it to me. He grabbed a t-shirt from his bag, put it on his head, wrapped it round, tucked some bits in and voilà, in ten seconds flat his entire face was covered apart from his eyes. I was impressed, but before I managed to tell him how impressive his demonstration was and then to get the thing off of his head he started shouting.

"What the fuck! Is that bitch a fucking paedo or something?!"

I was very confused and asked him what he was going on about as he pulled the t-shirt from his head.

"That fucking bitch just took a photo of me," he said as he pointed at the door.

I looked at the door and Rachel, the temporary behaviour support manager, was walking away from my door. I was baffled, what the hell had I missed, the other students in the class were getting agitated too and assured me that Rachel had indeed taken a photo through the door window. Zabir was furious.

"Wait until I tell my dad that this fucking paedo bitch is taking photos of me without my permission!" He raged.

It was the end of the day's final lesson and the students were due to leave, so I managed to calm him and the others down somewhat and they all went home. Once all of the other classes had left the school I immediately went looking for Rachel but found that she too had gone home, the situation would have to wait until the morning.

The following morning during the daily staff meeting, when asked if anybody has any announcements or information to share Rachel decided to pipe up. Now Rachel was your archetypal working-class posing as a middle-class, white woman in her late thirties and was brought in on a temporary contract to cover for Natalie who was on maternity leave. For some reason, she thought she was the dog's bollocks, but the truth is that she was only a flea's fart less annoying than Super Teacher (who was her new bestie). Rachel took any and every opportunity she had to try and demonstrate that she was highly intelligent (she wasn't), had the students' behaviour under control (she didn't), was adored by the students (she wasn't) and had some kind of authority over the other staff because her job title had the word manager in it (she didn't). In true Super Teacher style, Rachel slid her glasses to the end of her nose and peered over the top of them as she made her statement.

"Yesterday I had to put a safeguarding form in for Zabir, he is showing signs of religious extremism and we could be looking at potential ISIS radicalisation. I don't know if you have all read his file but his mother is from Afghanistan, this is serious and we need to remain vigilant. If anybody sees or hears anything you need to report it to me immediately so I can build a profile."

The room was stunned into near silence, all around were little whispers of either disbelief, confusion or concern.

She continued. "Luckily, I managed to get some evidence yesterday during Mr Foe's lesson but I can't be everywhere so you all need to be watching and listening."

All eyes immediately turned to me, the entire room waiting for me to divulge the tales of a terrorist in the making. I cleared my throat to speak and the room leaned in.

"Rachel, the next time you decide to take a photo of a student through my classroom window, don't. You thoroughly pissed Zabir and the rest of the group off yesterday and it took me the rest of the lesson to calm them all down again. Zabir has told me that he is going to ask his parents to put in a complaint about you because he thinks you're a paedophile as you took a photo of him without his permission. I managed to convince him to let me find out the full story before he did that, but understandably he's pretty annoyed and deserves an apology."

Rachel, looked at me like she was trying to calculate pi to one thousand decimal places in her head as I continued.

"Do you know why Zabir had that t-shirt over his head? No, you don't. Did you open the door and ask? Nope, just whipped out your phone and took a picture. Did you not think that if he was doing something wrong that I would have said something to him? I guess not, so instead, you decided to undermine me and create an actual problem for me to deal with right at the end of the day."

"Umm, ok I think we should have this conversation privately," she murmured sheepishly.

"So what was he doing then?" Asked Kate.

"I'm glad you asked. He was showing me how Dion used his t-shirt as a balaclava in a music video because I couldn't figure out how it was done when he was explaining it to me verbally," I then turned to face Rachel, "so you might want to find him before the first lesson starts and apologise Rachel, but be careful because at the moment he just thinks you're a paedophile but when he comes to the conclusion that you were being racist, well... You've read his file; he might just fuck you up."

FUCK YOU! FUCK THIS! OH FUCK!

Parents showing up at the PRU without their child's knowledge was often eye-opening in several ways. We went through a phase where if a student was having a particularly bad day and was causing massive amounts of disruption to everybody, we would call the student's parents without telling them and invite them to come down to the school so that they could witness their little angel behaving like a complete and utter prick in real-time. The strategy had two main objectives, the first was to dismantle the rose-tinted glasses that some parents had welded to their faces, which made them adamant that their child was a sweet, innocent, misunderstood saint who was being corrupted and scapegoated by the spawns of Satan that surrounded them in our school, because no matter what their child did they would never accept that their child was in the wrong. The other was to eliminate the possibility for a child to claim that the staffs' account of what happened was either an over-exaggeration or complete falsification, because as much as some of the students liked to act like they were fearless gangsters, they knew that their parents would be mortified and give them a thorough bollocking if they witnessed them behaving in the ways that they regularly did. Having said that, there were three common reactions from students when a parent arrived unexpectedly to the school, all of which can be attributed to the acute stress responses initially theorised by Walter Cannon in 1920, they are fight, flight and freeze or as I prefer to refer to them at the PRU, the 'Fuck You! Fuck This! and Oh Fuck!' responses.

The 'Fuck You!' response was elegantly demonstrated by a year nine girl named Zara. Now Zara wasn't the brightest student but she was always friendly, at least to me anyway. She was permanently excluded from her school for persistent disruptive behaviour, but to be fair to her she had just found out that her mother was not actually her biological mother. Zara was adopted at a very early age and had been lied to about it for over an entire decade. I guess that kind of mind fuckery isn't going to just dissipate so you can focus on studying for your GCSEs.

Zara was a master of work avoidance, she would flat out refuse to do any work, ever. She would spend pretty much every minute of her school day sitting on the floor in corridors refusing to even go into a classroom and sit down. We had tried everything we could think of to get her into her lessons; rewards, sanctions, bribes, changing groups, planned ignoring and God knows what else but nothing was working. After calling her mother every other day to inform her of her daughter's lack of engagement, Zara's mother decided to put her foot down.

"Right that's it, tomorrow I'm coming to the school and I'll put her in the lessons myself." She told us with undisputable confidence. "Trust me she will do as she's told."

In the staff room, this was all anybody was talking about, a few of us were sceptical as to how effective she would be but when someone mentioned that her mother was a police sergeant, minds started to change. Oh shit, this is going to be good, we thought. A parent who is actually going to take serious action with their child, not only that, she's a police sergeant, we could not wait until the following day.

The next day Zara came into school and was up to her usual antics, she sat in the corridor refusing to go to her first two lessons and then at break time her mother turned up. Zara was outside smoking a cigarette with her friends when news reached her that her mom was in the reception area. Zara finished her cigarette and went off to the reception area to see if the gossip was true. Knowing what her mom had said on the phone previously, a few members of staff, myself included went to go and see Zara's response to her mom's unexpected arrival, as did a bunch of the students who again could not wait to see Zara's reaction.

Zara walked through the door to reception and saw her mom stood talking to Liz, the headteacher. Zara's mother looked like The Trunchbull from the movie Matilda, she was tall, stocky, wore no makeup and had her hair tied up in a scruffy bun. She stood like she was in the military with her back straight, shoulders back and chin up, that police officer vibe of assumed authority and superiority leaked from her demeanour like grease from a pricked sausage, none of which seemed to phase Zara.

"Why are you here?" Zara said with potent disdain and confusion.

"I'm here to sit with you, in your lessons Zara," her mom responded with half a smirk before returning to a stern face.

Zara did the exact same smirk and then serious look before she spoke.

"Well that's not gonna happen 'cause I'm not going to lessons, so you might as well go back home."

"Hmmm, no Zara," she said while looking at the crowd of people stood around, she then looked down at Zara and with a slight nod and forced laugh, "you're going to your lesson."

"No, I'm not, now shut the fuck up and go back home." Zara retorted immediately.

The crowd was growing with each interaction and we all stood waiting for Zara's mom to literally lay down the law and frog-march Zara into her first lesson in months.

"Listen if I have to come down here and embarrass you in front of everybody here," she gestured with her hand to the ever-growing audience, "so that you go to your lessons, well so be it. I'm more than happy to do that."

Zara didn't say a word for a few seconds, she just looked at her mother like she wanted to slap her in the face, thankfully she didn't but what she did do was deliver the most devastating comeback I've ever heard a student give to a parent.

"Embarrass me? I'll embarrass you! You big twat, because

I'm not the one who doesn't know how to clear the search history after looking for videos of big black cocks on the laptop. D'ya really wanna sit in lessons with me? While I tell everyone what other shit you've been looking at? With your massive purple vibrator on top of the wardrobe, you fucking tramp!"

It was at that point the headteacher thought it's probably best to disperse the crowd that had gathered and tell everyone to go off to their next lesson.

Now to be fair to Zara's mom, she did stay for the rest of the day and try and get her daughter into lessons, however unsuccessfully, but to be honest, even if she did succeed that still wouldn't have been the thing that everyone was talking about for the rest of the week.

The 'Fuck This!' response was best demonstrated by a year eight boy called Jacob Bishop. Jacob was funny and looked all cute and innocent, he was absolutely tiny and could have passed for a year five student. Jacob had been at the school for a few weeks and was the fourth of his eight siblings to attend the PRU. The school near to their home that their parents sent them to routinely booted the Bishops out just as the last one was leaving the PRU, ensuring that we always had at least one Bishop on our roll at all times. We joked that the school would top us up with Bishops like credit on an old pay as you go sim, as this is how it often felt. His older sister Jane had attended a few years prior and as she left us in year eleven we had her younger brother Johnathan being kicked out and sent to us in year eight. When he reached year eleven, Jacob was kicked out and sent to us (and in case you were wondering as I once did, yes all of the siblings had names beginning with J).

Anyway, if I had to use one word to describe Jacob it would be feral, if I had to use two words I'd say completely feral, for the most accurate description, however, I would require three words and they would be feral as fuck. He seemed like he had been pretty much left to raise himself or more likely been brought up by his older siblings who themselves were feral children, like the lost boys in Peter Pan, hence the reason his sister showed up to the school to witness his behaviour as opposed to his mom or dad.

Jacob had climbed out of the English classroom window and was throwing stones over the fence at the back of the school, he was trying to smash some windows on the houses in the distance (just for fun), when his sister showed up. As she walked out onto the playground Jacob was stood with his arm cranked right back as he prepared to launch his next stone.

"Oi you little shit!" Shouted Janet.

Startled by his sister's voice Jacob let out a little scream, dropped the stones in his hands turned around and ran as fast as he could. We walked around the corner to call Jacob back but he was nowhere to be seen. We walked around the school grounds, inside and out but could not find him anywhere. After searching for half an hour we assumed he'd left the school grounds and his sister went home to see if he had gone there. Roughly an hour later his sister called the school to inform us that Jacob had not been home and wondered if we had seen him yet, which we hadn't.

At the end of the school day, a further hour or so later I and a few other members of staff were dismissing the students, as we stood in the car park and watched the students head off up the road we saw a foot appear from underneath the minibus, then a leg, then an arm and eventually an entire Jacob emerge from underneath the minibus covered in mud and grease. He rose to his feet started jogging to catch up with his friend.

"Jacob!" I shouted as he brushed himself off, "have you been under the minibus all this time?"

Jacob turned around and whilst continuing to run backwards he smiled, put his finger to his lips, shushed and nodded his head. He then turned back around and continued running whilst holding his middle finger high in the air at me.

The 'Oh Fuck!' response was most frequently demonstrated with unsettling perfection by Kingsley whenever his dad showed up to school, but a more hilarious example of the 'Oh Fuck!' response came from a boy called Richard after his parents arrived at a science lesson to find their beloved boy throwing equipment around the science classroom and swearing at the teacher.

Richard was in year eleven, he was by far the biggest kid in the school and would constantly be using his size to intimidate other students. He was about six feet tall and weighed at least eighteen stone. Richard was clearly overindulged by his parents and this was evident not only by his weight but also by his constant bragging and flaunting about how much money or expensive items he owned.

Richard would arrive at school every day with a thick solid gold bracelet that weighed at least two ounces, a gold chain that probably weighed another two ounces and everything he wore was a designer label. He would always have at least fifty pounds in cash on him when we emptied his pockets in the morning, which he would literally shake in front of students' faces to make certain that everybody knew about it.

So Richard was in his science lesson being a tosser, literally, he was tossing test tubes and other equipment around the room. He was refusing to complete any work and when asked by the teacher, Lucas, to make even the slightest effort he was responding with an array of aggressive and abusive commentary. Upon arrival at the school, Richard's parents were taken to the corridor outside of the science classroom where they heard Lucas asking Richard for what felt like the one-millionth time to do his work.

"C'mon Richard just stick the learning objective in your book and have a look at the questions please?"

"Go fuck yourself enit, I told you already I ent doin' ya shitty fucking questions," Richard grumbled back.

"What if this comes up on the GCSE paper Richard? Which it most likely will. Look, you haven't got to write the answers down I just need you to look at the questions" Lucas pleaded.

Richard's parents walked up to the classroom window where they could see Richard sat with his back to them, Richard picked his book up from the table and skimmed it like a Frisbee across the room.

"Fam, fuck off with ya fucking questions. I couldn't give a

fuck about a science GCSE, ya get me?"

Richard looked at the other students with a smirk on his face, however, the smirk quickly morphed into a look of utter fear and embarrassment when the door opened, his parents walked in and he heard his mom call his name.

"Richard! Go and pick that book up right now!" She yelled.

Richard turned around and before he could even get his head around what was happening his Dad just unleashed utter fury.

"PICK UP THE BOOK! PICK IT UP NOW BEFORE I BEAT YOU TO DEATH WITH IT! PICK IT UP!" His voice boomed.

Richard leapt from his chair and ran across the room to retrieve his book.

"I cannot. Believe. What I have just heard from you in here Richard. The way that you have spoken to your teacher. Absolutely... disgusting!" His mom said slowly and with vigour.

Richard, all flustered handed the book to his mom for some reason.

"WHAT ARE YOU GIVING IT TO HER FOR?!" Screamed his dad as the veins protruded from his head. "SIT DOWN!"

Richard quickly sat in his chair, avoiding eye contact with the other students who were at this point silent and not moving at all, partly because they too probably didn't want a roasting from Richard's furious father.

"Say sorry to your..." said his mother as she pointed at

Lucas.

Richard rapidly complied with the request before she could finish her sentence. Richard's father was pacing in and out of the door clearly still enraged.

"Why haven't you been doing what your teacher asks you to do?" Asked his mother calmly but firmly.

Richard lifted his head to meet her gaze and replied softly, "I don't like science mom, so what's the point in even listening to him?"

Richard's dad exploded again, "BECAUSE HE'S THE FUCK-ING TEACHER! NOW SHUT UP AND SIT DOWN PROPPER BE-FORE I SIT YOU DOWN! I swear to God boy if I EVER hear that you are being this disrespectful again, oh your feet won't touch the bloody floor mark my words!"

Richard sat down, stuck the learning objective in his book and stared at the list of questions. To prevent Richard's dad from either committing homicide or bursting a vein in his head, the headteacher decided that the point had been made and it was time to show the parents out.

WHY ARE YOU IGNORING ME?!

Tara joined us in year nine and did not stop talking from the second she arrived. To call her an attention seeker would be an understatement, she craved attention all of the time and when she didn't get it, she was relentless in pursuing it. Tara's best friend was also at the PRU and had joined us a few months before her, her name was Isobel and all of the boys were instantly infatuated with her.

Isobel dressed like women on hen nights or at costume parties do when they dress up as schoolgirls for a night out. She was naturally pretty but also would not be seen in school without a full face of makeup, fake eyelashes and nails (maybe fake hair too, I'm not sure), she wore a short skirt with those long socks that go over the knees and a partially buttoned shirt which she was constantly being told to button up properly. As she was getting all of the attention from the boys (and the other girls albeit for reasons of jealousy) Tara quickly adopted the exact same look, although it certainly did not have the same effect on the other students, she clearly did this for the attention.

Tara would be considered highly intelligent if she was a chimpanzee but as far as I could tell she was indeed a human, so this was never going to be the case. I have no doubt in my mind that if she ever figures out how to access an email account there will be a plethora of very happy Nigerian princes roaming around Africa, which leads nicely onto my next point.

Tara thought that Africa was a country, I can see how this might be an easy mistake to make and it was far from the dumbest thing I've heard a fourteen-year-old say. What made it ludicrous and not easily forgiven was that when other students and staff correctly informed her that Africa was a continent and not a country, she was having none of it. They Googled it and even showed her on a map but she still refused to believe it and was adamant that everybody, including Google and a map of the world were lying to her, as if a giant conspiracy had been orchestrated with the sole purpose of misleading her on this one insignificant fact.

My favourite example of how her mind worked (or didn't) is, she was once trying to push past Roger, the assistant headteacher, to get through a door that she didn't need to go through. When he wouldn't let her through she started viciously swearing at him. In response to her foul language, Roger told her that swearing at him was like 'water off a duck's back' to him and from that comment she became convinced that he was attempting to drown ducks. She was so sure of it that she went into her

English lesson outraged and decided to share her findings with the rest of the group.

"I think you teachers are all cruel, Roger said that he was going to drown a duck! Can ducks get drownded?"

Slightly puzzled by what was happening John, the English teacher replied.

"Drownded is not a word."

Before he could squeeze out another word Tara responded.

"Shut up, you're being racist!"

How she got to that conclusion is anyone's guess. Clearly confused and unwilling to get into a huge debate about the nonsense tumbling from her tongue, John then asked her to sit down and do her work. Tara, however, had more important things to do, she felt compelled to write a letter to the RSPCA informing them of the atrocity that was taking place concerning the improper treatment and potential murder of ducks.

So yes, Tara said ridiculously ignorant and idiotic things all of the time, which I could get over pretty swiftly but what I couldn't handle was that she was just constantly talking and wouldn't shut the fuck up for more than five seconds. I used to have her group for a triple lesson on a Monday morning and fucking hell it was the most excruciating way to start the week. By lesson three even the students were sick of her.

One day during the third of the three lessons, Isobel mentioned something about how she would never let her boyfriend have a girl as a friend and that if he did have one she would consider it cheating, she then asked me if my partner and I felt the same way. This question sparked an interesting debate among the group, so I decided that we were no longer going to punish ourselves with three lessons of ICT and I got all of the students and the teaching assistant into a circle so that we could discuss Isobel's comment. We were passing a ball around the group, the idea being only the person with the ball is allowed to speak thus ensuring that everyone is heard. Unsurprisingly, this wasn't sitting well with Tara who was blabbering relentlessly as usual. After repeatedly asking her to stop interrupting, I and the rest of the group, including her bestie, were getting annoyed.

"Alright, that's enough now Tara, if you keep on shouting out and interrupting then I'm keeping you behind after school because this is just getting ridiculous." I told her.

Obviously, my warning was not heeded and she continued to ramble on. After another five minutes of her verbal dysentery, I was so tired of addressing it that I decided to completely ghost her to see if she'd stop talking, very quickly the rest of the class realised what I was doing and decided to do the same. As people were no longer responding to her comments and continuing to participate with the conversation as if she was not there she started to get frustrated.

"Are you all ignoring me?" She asked.

Tara's question was acknowledged by nobody, she looked around at everyone trying to figure out what was happening.

"Are you ignoring me?" She enquired again.

Still, everybody continued with the discussion and paid no

attention to Tara.

"Umm hello, why are you all ignoring me?" She said abruptly. "STOP IGNORING ME!"

Again there was no response from anybody, Tara looked at everybody in a panic and shouted again.

"Why are you ignoring me?! Why are you ignoring me?! WHY ARE YOU IGNORING ME?!" She screamed as loud as she could, "WHY ARE YOU IGNORING ME?! WHY ARE YOU IGNORING ME?! WHY ARE YOU IGNORING ME?!"

Tara was screaming so loud that Roger, who was in his office with the door closed, at least thirty metres away at the other end of the corridor, came to the classroom to investigate what the hell was going on. He opened the classroom door to find Tara who was still screaming as loud as humanly possible.

"WHY ARE YOU IGNORING ME?!"

Roger looked at us all sat in a circle having a calm and relaxed chat while Tara continued screaming.

"You alright sir?" He asked calmly.

"Yes thanks, we're all good." I replied.

Tara let out another chorus of WHY ARE YOU IGNORING ME?! And once again I and the rest of the group ignored her and carried on with our conversation.

"WHY IS HE IGNORING ME?!" Tara yelled at Roger.

To be honest, I was expecting him to tell her to get out of

the room and go with him to his office because she was disrupting not only my class but all of the others on the same corridor, but instead, he did something even better... he completely ignored her.

"I just came to let you know that we've cancelled the staff meeting tonight, so as soon as the students are out you can go."

Tara started looking around rapidly in a frenzy, desperate to make eye contact with someone, she even looked at her hands for a second like she was checking that they were still there and that she hadn't all of a sudden turned invisible or started to disappear like Marty McFly.

"SIRRRR HE'S IGNORING MEEEE!!" Tara screamed with upset and urgency.

"Ok cheers Roger, thanks for letting us know," I said.

Roger closed the door and off he went back to his office.

"URRRGH! I DON'T LIKE YOU! YOU'RE A BASTARD TEACHER!" Tara screamed as she stormed out of the classroom slamming the door shut behind her.

At the end of the school day, as the students were lined up to be dismissed, I told Tara that she needed to come and speak to me for ten minutes about her behaviour in my lesson before she left. Clearly still very annoyed with me, she told me to fuck off and that she would not be coming to speak to me. Of course, I expected this response but there was no way I was willing to let her go home without discussing her behaviour before she left. I immediately went down to the reception area and collected her mobile phone from the office, I took it back to my classroom and locked it in my cupboard but ensured that it was in full view from the window on the door. I then walked back down to Tara who was nearing the front of the line.

"Tara I need to speak to you in my classroom, it will only be five or ten minutes and then you can go home."

"How about fuck off, I'm not talking to you and I'm never going to your classroom ever again," she said as she scrunched up her face at me like a five-year-old.

"Ok, Tara I'll see you in a minute, just come down to my classroom when you're ready ok?" I said over-enthusiastically and confident with a big smile on my face.

Tara stuck her middle finger up at me and I went to my classroom. Twenty minutes later Tara arrived at my classroom escorted by Christine, the headteacher. She stood with her arms crossed and sulking like a little kid who had been denied ice cream. She looked so pissed off that it was absolutely hilarious. I was trying my hardest not to laugh but wasn't doing a great job of it, my lip quivered as I tried to hold it in. Christine was also trying not to laugh but was doing a much better job than I was.

"Where's my phone?" She said grumpily with her head down and shoulders sunk.

I pointed to the door and she looked and saw her phone through the window, she tried to open the door and realised it was locked. She then started to rattle the handle.

"Urrrgh, give me my phone, I'm going home!" She moaned.

"Sit down for five minutes and talk to me and I'll get it after," I said calmly.

"No! Give me my phone now!" she said angrily.

I didn't say anything else I just gestured towards the chair that I wanted her to sit in with an open palm and sat waiting for her to sit down. In the end, Christine pretty much placed her in the chair and then I said what I had to say. The entire conversation was over in five minutes, I explained to her why I ignored her and what the expectations were regarding her behaviour moving forward, then I gave Tara her phone back and she left.

Ever since that day Tara never ever came back to one of my lessons, instead she would stand outside in the corridor and tell everybody who asked her to go into the classroom that she wouldn't because I was horrible to her. Logically they would then ask what I had done, thinking it was something I'd done on that day or at least that week and Tara would tell them all about how I was the bastard teacher that kept her behind, conveniently omitting the part where she screamed 'why are you ignoring me?' for thirty minutes straight I might add. Even six months later, every time I saw Tara in a hallway or anywhere else in school she would turn to whoever was nearby, staff or student and say 'I hate him, he's the bastard teacher who kept me behind after school.'

The strangest part about this is that I actually got to know Tara pretty well from having conversations with her outside of my classroom and she was alright at times, problematic and unconfident, but was a loyal friend and had good banter. It was obvious to everyone who spoke to her or saw me speaking to her that she didn't actually hate me, but she had now found herself in this weird situation where she had been telling everybody that she hated me for so long that she'd gone passed the point of no return. If she changed her mind at any point it would make her feel as though she'd somehow lost and I had won. Also, this way garnered more attention from people... Which she loved.

ANIL'S DAD AIN'T NUTTIN TA FUCK WIT!

We took all of the students on a camping trip for a few days. When we arrived the students' moods matched the weather, both were pretty miserable, it was cold and raining ever so slightly. Most of the staff were helping students to put up their tents as quickly as possible and a lot of them were really struggling. After helping a few students to put their tents up I noticed two year eight boys sat in the minibus, one was a new student called J.R. who had only been with us for a couple of weeks, so I didn't know him very well. The other was a boy called Anil who I knew well and was often problematic.

Anil was very silly and immature even for a year eight, and often did stupid things that he shouldn't be doing, however, he was not very bright and always got caught. He was not actually supposed to be on the camping trip but Roger decided to let him join us as he didn't want him to miss out on the experience. Anil had recently been on a fixed-term exclusion for prank calling the school, he used an app on his phone to convince the receptionist that there was a problem with the water at the school. I don't know the exact details but he basically told her that it was contaminated in some way, prompting her to call a technician from the water company to come and do some emergency testing. He got found out almost immediately afterwards however because being the genius James Bond villain that he was, he sat in the reception area bragging about his prank to his friends while a member of staff listened to him from the other side of the door. Not only that but he was also sat under a CCTV camera which recorded the whole thing.

Anil was a small boy in both height and weight, he had short black hair with a tramline shaved into the side and wore a black Nike tracksuit everywhere he went. His voice was unbroken and shrill, which got worse when he threw his tantrums as was often the case. Anil was the youngest in his household and came from an affluent family where his mother spoilt him with any and everything he wanted to keep him happy, something he bragged about constantly to his peers, much to their annoyance. His latest indulgence was the latest iPhone which he did not shut up about and pulled out at every opportunity to flaunt in front of the other students.

I walked over to the minibus, opened the door and asked them to get out of the vehicle and to go and sort out their tents, they both got out of the minibus and sat in front of it on the floor of the gravel-covered car park.

"Fuck off I ent doing no tent, camping is shit." Anil moaned.

The two boys then decided it'd be a great idea to pick up small stones and throw them at the cars in the car park. After asking them multiple times to stop they both began to complain.

"This is fucking shit, I wanna go home!" They moaned like a pair of foul-mouthed toddlers.

After a couple of minutes of trying to talk them round, one of the teaching assistants called Beth went and informed the assistant headteacher, Roger, of the two boys' behaviour. Roger was on the field and shouted over to the boys who were at this point hurling stones at the minibus.

"Boys if you damage any vehicles here your parents will be billed and I don't think that will go down too well. Just give camping a chance, we've only just arrived, come here and I will help you to put your tents up."

Anil sat on the floor looking like someone had just pissed in his milkshake.

"Tell my dad I don't care; he won't give a shit!" He said as he threw another stone at the cars.

I sat down next to Anil on the floor and said softly, "Anil that's enough now, stop throwing stones because you will damage someone's car in a minute and your parents will end up getting the bill, I don't want you to get in any trouble."

Anil laughed. "A bill for that piece of shit car, my iPhone's worth more than that car, that car's probably worth a fucking pound. My dad would laugh at you if you tried to give him a bill for that."

J.R., being encouraged to join in by Anil continued attempting to throw stones at the cars, however each time he attempted to pick up a stone I managed to either knock it from his hand or prevent him from picking one up altogether. Seeing what was going on, Roger came over to the boys.

"If you want to go home that badly then fine, get in the people carrier and I'll take you home because I can't have you here throwing stones at the vehicles."

Now most students at this point would be like 'great I got what I wanted' and get in the car, but not Anil. This fucking idiot picked up a big rock, about the size of a tennis ball, screamed I wanna go home! Then attempted to throw it at the very car he was going to be taken home in. Roger, quickly caught hold of Anil's forearm and removed the rock from his hand and whilst doing so Anil decided to kick him as hard as he could in the shin. Seeing that things were getting a little out of control I went over and took control of Anil's other arm and we put him into a single elbow hold (a restraint technique taught by companies like Team-Teach and Prime) we walked Anil to the people carrier and put him in the back seat.

As we were getting Anil into the car Roger said, "Anil your dad is not going to be happy with this behaviour when I speak to him is he? You've damaged people's property and physically assaulted me."

"Tell my fucking dad, do you think he's going to listen to you. He'll tell you to fuck off." Anil responded.

I was sat in the back of the car with Anil while Roger went

and got in the driver's seat. Beth told J.R. to get in the back row of the car and put his seatbelt on which he did without question. Anil then decided that he would begin kicking the back of the driver's seat where Roger was sat and refused to put his seatbelt on.

"I wanna go home!" He cried again.

"Where do you think we are taking you?" I asked calmly, "you're going home but we can't drive anywhere until you put your seatbelt on, just stop kicking the chair and put your belt on so we can go."

Like a broken record Anil screamed again, "I wanna go home!"

Again he then began to kick Roger's chair as hard as possible. Unable to drive while being booted in the back by a disorderly thirteen-year-old, Roger called Beth over and asked her to drive the car while he jumped in the back and sat on the other side of Anil. We drove all the way back down the motorway holding Anil in his seat in a seated double elbow hold whilst he screamed to people in the cars next to us 'Help! I'm being kidnapped!' Since nobody could hear him or seemed to care about the alleged kidnapping that was unfolding in the car parallel to them, Anil told J.R. to kick the back window through. Not wanting to disappoint his newfound master, J.R. began kicking the window as hard as possible attempting to break it while doing seventy miles per hour down the M42, all the while screaming for help.

I had loosened my hold of Anil's arm slightly because he

was not being aggressive towards me but Roger maintained a firmer grip on the other side because he was continuously trying to attack him. Anil then began kicking and scraping the heel of his trainers down Roger's shin, while doing so he was shouting 'Let go of my arm ya fat cunt' and 'Watch when we get to school my dad is gonna knock you out.' Roger, although clearly in pain remained calm.

"Anil you need to stop hurting me," he said, "your dad will be at the school waiting to pick you up and you are just adding more things to the list of things I'm going to have to tell him about your behaviour."

"I don't give a fuck, tell my dad what you want he'll laugh in your face, then he's gonna knock you out for holding me in this car you fucking paedo!"

Beth had already contacted the school and arranged for Anil's dad to meet us there, to discuss what had happened and to collect his son to go home, so when we arrived he met us at the vehicle as we pulled into the car park. Upon seeing his dad Anil put on a BAFTA Award winning performance, it was un-fucking-believable. He immediately began to sob, professing that we and more specifically Roger had hurt his arm when holding him in his seat. He claimed that he wasn't doing anything wrong and that he just asked to go home because he didn't like camping. Anil's dad was clearly extremely pissed off, his fists were clenched and his face was getting redder and redder by the second. He turned to Roger and took a step towards him.

"So what's happened then? Because I've had to leave work for this and I am not bloody happy."

Roger then told him everything that had happened, he told him about the stone-throwing, the kicking of the chair, the verbal abuse and then he pointed to the marks on his leg where Anil had been scraping and kicking him. Anil's dad turned to his son and looked at him with fiery eyes.

"Did you do this?" He said, pointing at Roger's leg.

"Yeah but..."

Anil's dad held out his hand and sternly said a single word.

"Phone."

Anil reluctantly took his brand new iPhone from his pocket and gently placed it into his dad's palm like a delicate flower. Instantly after receiving the phone Anil's dad then threw it as hard as he could straight onto the pavement, pieces of the phone exploded off in all directions like a firework. Anil let out a screaming cry as he dropped to his knees like he'd just been shot in the leg. He picked up his phone and held it in his cupped hands like a dying bird, looking at it in complete shock and horror.

"Get in the car. Now!" Yelled his dad.

Anil struggled to his feet as the tears trickled from his chin like a leaky tap. Mourning the loss of his iPhone he slowly got into his dad's Mercedes and the two of them zoomed out of the car park to the sound of Wu-Tang Clan Ain't Nuttin ta Fuck Wit.

Roger, Beth and I all got back in the car and sat in silence for a few seconds, J.R. was sat quietly in the back.

"Right J.R.," said Beth "Where do you live? We'll drop you

back home."

EARN THE WIN

We were taking some key stage four students to the gym for a PE lesson, one of whom was a year ten boy called D'Quan. D'Quan was a chubby kid but he had that delusional mindset that some male chunkers tend have, you know the one where they convince themselves that really they are muscly for some reason. He thought and acted like he was the toughest kid in the world (unless you call his mom and tell her he's being kept behind because he refused to read a book, then he cries like a little bitch) and was constantly going on about how he could beat everybody in a fight, including me.

In the gym I had the students gathered around me so I could show them the correct techniques when lifting different weights and doing different exercises, as it was a demonstration I was using very light weights so that I could talk and explain things easily as I went through the information that they needed to know. Seeing me lift the lighter weights was for some reason hilarious to D'Quan, who proceeded to call me a pussy and claim that he was stronger than me. Now I hadn't been to the gym in about a year at this point but when I did go I took it very seriously, strict routine, strict diet, all that shit (I may have been a bit of an addict). I obviously was much stronger back then but even being out of training for a while, being a fully grown fucking adult meant that I was clearly stronger than this Pillsbury Doughboy.

I decided to ignore D'Quan and continued with the demonstrations as we went around different equipment. Each time I gave a demonstration D'Quan would giggle and make some comment about how weak I was and how much stronger he was than me. All of the other students kept on telling him that he was deluded and that it was clear that I could do more but was just giving advice and guidance on how to use the equipment safely, but D'Quan continued and just would not shut up. By the time we were halfway around the gym, I was beginning to get annoyed with his constant interrupting, giggling and comments.

"Ok D'Quan, you're starting to annoy me now. If you really think you're stronger than me, point to a piece of equipment and we'll see what you've got."

To be completely honest I thought that this would be enough for him to tuck his tail and shut the fuck up, but no, D'Quan pointed to the pull-up bar.

"Come on then, pull-ups," he said eagerly.

I stood there for a few seconds waiting for him to retract his proposal, but he didn't he kept pointing over and over again at the pull-up bar. My eyes widened as I began looking around at the rest of the students checking their faces to see if I had missed something, I could not believe it, he actually believed that he could win this challenge. The look of shock on my face was clear but D'Quan seemed to think that this was a look of fear, he thought I feared losing the challenge as opposed to being genuinely stunned that he actually thought he was stronger than me.

"Ahhh look you're shitting it now Foe, ent ya?" He said.

"Oh yeah definitely." I sarcastically replied.

I walked over to the pull-up bar and all of the students gathered around.

"Ok do as many as you can and I'll beat it," I said to him.

"No, YOU go first and I'LL beat it," he responded.

I couldn't be bothered to do a shit load of pull-ups, I just wanted to do enough that I knew he wouldn't beat. I looked him up and down trying to estimate in my head how many he might be able to do.

"I'm just going to do five because I don't even think you'll manage that, if you do then I'll do another five and we'll keep going. Five each until someone gives up, yeah?"

All of the students gathered around while I did five pull-ups. I dropped down from the bar and looked at D'Quan.

"You're up."

D'Quan strolled up to the bar with the swagger of a pimp from a seventies blaxploitation movie, he jumped up grabbed onto the bar and hung there. We all waited for him to lift himself and... Nothing happened, he just hung there.

"Go on then!" Shouted the other students.

The slightest bend appeared in the creases of his elbows as he tried desperately to lift himself to no avail. His arms began to quiver and his head writhed side to side as he strained, his moans and groans crept out of his clenched teeth like he was constipated and trying to squeeze out a monster shit. He hung there for about thirty seconds while the other students switched from uncontrollable laughter to embarrassment on his behalf and told him to give up. D'Quan eventually surrendered to gravity, letting go of the bar and falling to the floor.

"Wow... Well, that's that then." I said bluntly and walked away.

I managed to move about five paces before D'Quan piped up once more.

"That doesn't mean anything, I'm still stronger than you."

"Ok, whatever D'Quan."

"I am, let's do something else then."

"D'Quan, you've already embarrassed yourself enough, just take the L and move on." I said as I continued around the gym.

For the next half hour, D'Quan continued to try and convince everybody that he was stronger than me and constantly challenged me to lift the most weights on each machine. Every time, I told him no because if he gets injured trying to lift weights that are too heavy for him I didn't want anything to do with it. Not only was I saying this to him but the other students were also constantly telling him to give up and accept that he'd lost.

"Boxing, come let's box?" Said D'Quan.

"We're not boxing."

"Haaa pussy, you're scared, because you know I'm stronger than you."

"No D'Quan, because I'm your teacher and I'm not going to punch you in the face to prove a point. Use some common sense."

By now D'Quan had been going on and on so much that honestly, nothing would have made me feel better than putting on some boxing gloves and pummeling his face until he became the Elephant Man's doppelganger. I didn't actually care about proving anything to him I just wanted him to shut up.

We had about an hour left at the gym and we decided to go down to the sports hall and get some equipment out. Whilst waiting for the staff at the leisure centre to set up the badminton court on one side and get the football goals set up on the other D'Quan threw down another challenge.

"Race me then you pussy!"

"What?"

"Race me, I'll kill you in a race."

"Well, you should D'Quan, I smoked for longer than you've been alive."

"So let's race then."

"I can't be arsed to beat you again D'Quan, I know I'm faster than you, it's pretty obvious I'll win." i said unenthusiastically.

D'Quan stood on the line at the end of the hall and began stretching his legs. He then started to jog on the spot bringing his knees as high as he could like Usain Bolt warming up before he steps into the starting blocks. I looked at him out of the corner of my eye and shook my head.

"Don't shake your head, race me ya pussy."

"You know I'm a competitive guy D'Quan, so I'm not going to let you win... You know that yeah?" I said joining him on the line.

D'Quan looked around at the rest of the students with a smug smirk.

"Oh my days, listen to this dickhead ya know, like I can't beat him in a race and he's gonna let me win."

"No, I said I WON'T, let you win. So if you beat me, you know that you really did beat me. You've gotta earn the win D'Quan. Now, what are we doing, there and back or just to the other end?" I asked while pointing at the opposite wall.

"There and back."

"Alright let's go."

All of the other students gathered around once again and one of them counted down from three... two... one.

"Go!" They all shouted in unison.

For a second or two D'Quan kept up with me but then

quickly got left behind. I reached the other end of the hall and turned back to do the final length and saw D'Quan's gutted face as he realised that he had lost again.

"Fuck you! This is bullshit!" He whined.

D'Quan sat on the floor in the middle of the sports hall and sulked, so I stopped running and walked back up to the other students who were stood by the finish line.

"Who's doing what then people? If you wanna play football stay over this side and if anyone wants to have a game of badminton come over this side with me."

The other students, I think either felt sorry for D'Quan or just didn't even care anymore about his willingness to further embarrass himself and so they too just walked away without mentioning the race at all. Most of the boys went off to one side of the sports hall and began playing football and I was playing badminton with one of the girls on the other side of the sports hall.

I had been playing badminton with Harriet for less than two minutes, not competitively just seeing if we could keep a rally going, when once again D'Quan walked over to me.

"Urgh, you're shit at badminton Foe!" He said.

I didn't even look at him I just completely ignored him and carried on playing.

"You think you're good but you're actually quite shit sooo..."

Harriet was beginning to get annoyed with D'Quan

now, she was trying to concentrate on keeping the rally going but couldn't focus because of his constant shit-talking.

"D'Quan you've lost at everything, just shut up and fuck off man," she said candidly

"Umm whatever, I mean like yeah he might be a little bit faster than me and that but I actually am the best at badminton though sooo... It's about skill."

Harriet didn't respond to D'Quan she just handed him the racket, she then walked off of the court and stood on the sideline staring at him.

"Hurry up and beat him so he can fuck off and cry and we can carry on playing," she said with her arms folded.

"I can't be bothered to play him; I just want a little rally," I said with frustration.

"Just do it so he can fuck off and leave us alone."

"Yeah come on Foe you pussy, play me. Winner stays on unless you're scared 'cause you know you'll lose."

I was so annoyed that I didn't even set any rules or score limit for the game. I just served the shuttlecock to D'Quan, he returned it and as soon as it came back to me I smashed it as hard as I could to the ground before he even had the opportunity to move.

"One-nil!" I said pointing my racket at the shuttlecock.

D'Quan served the shuttlecock to me and once again I smashed it as hard as I could straight to the ground.

"Two-nil!"

D'Quan served again, and again I smashed it straight passed him to the floor.

"Three!"

Harriet started laughing at D'Quan as he snatched the shuttlecock up from the floor with frustration.

"You serve, you think you're good but it's just cause I'm serving all the time," said D'Quan.

D'Quan threw me the shuttlecock to serve, which I did straight over his head. He swung his badminton racket in the air multiple times like he was swatting invisible flies completely missing the shuttlecock. Harriet was stood on the sideline pissing herself laughing and calling everybody over to watch D'Quan being destroyed once again. It was clear to D'Quan that he had no chance of beating me and that I was in no way even giving him a chance at winning.

"Fuck you!" He shouted.

He launched his racket across the sports hall and stormed off of the court, angrily kicking his bottle of Volvic across the floor as he left.

About six months later we were at school and the new P.E. teacher, Greg, had set up a badminton court in the hall. I was playing with some of the students seeing if we could keep a rally going and once again D'Quan showed up talking shit. There were a lot of new staff and students around who were unaware of D'Quan's former efforts to beat me at sports and subsequent failure and humiliation. So when I refused to play him they all assumed it was because I was afraid to lose, especially given his confident rhetoric. I told them all that I was refusing to play him because I knew he could not take losing but nobody cared. One of the students handed D'Quan a racket so I immediately handed mine to Greg and walked off of the court.

"Aaah see everyone, he's scared to play me!" Laughed D'Quan.

Greg held the racket out towards me.

"Just play him, Sir, first to seven."

"No, he can't take losing, I've played him before and he pretty much cried when he lost."

"Just let him win then. Don't make it obvious though." He whispered.

By now there were quite a few members of staff and students gathering around to watch. They were all pestering me to play him and D'Quan was continuing to run his mouth about how much he was going to annihilate me at badminton. I took the racket and started to play. It was fairly even for the first few points and then D'Quan took the lead, the score was five to four. D'Quan was getting more and more cocky and loud with every point he scored and more people gathered to watch.

"Urgh Foe you little pussy, I told you you're shit."

"And what did I tell you D'Quan? You've gotta earn the win."

I switched the racket from my left to my right hand with

extremely slow and exaggerated movement so that it was clear to everybody including D'Quan that I was not actually left-handed, I could see the look of realisation in his face, the flash-backs from his last soul-crushing defeat racing through his mind. He served the shuttlecock and as before I smashed the shuttlecock as hard as I could straight past him at lightning speed. He hesitantly picked up the shuttlecock as it dawned on him that he once again had no chance of winning. He served again and once again I smashed the shuttlecock to the ground before he even managed to move.

"Matchpoint," I said smugly.

D'Quan gave me the shuttlecock to serve. I served it short and he stretched forward to return it almost falling over in the process. The shuttlecock rose high in the air and I took a couple of steps back before finally smashing it straight at his feet. D'Quan swung the racket wildly completely missing the shuttle-cock once again. He stood in silence staring at the luminous yellow plastic and white cork lay at his feet. I walked to the net with my hand out to shake his hand and just as he did before he threw his racket across the hall.

"Fuck you man!" He sulked.

Greg picked up the racket to check it wasn't damaged before walking over to me.

"I thought you were going to let him win." He said dis-creetly in my ear.

"Nah fuck that," I quietly replied as I handed the racket to him, "he's gotta earn the win."

MARVIN FOE

AFTERWORD

Over my many years of teaching, I have found myself in all sorts of situations which have taken me through the entire emotional spectrum. I regularly talk to my friends and family (some of whom also work in education) about some of the scenarios that I have found myself in, or conversations that I have had with students and staff to find them sitting on the edge of their seats with dropped jaws, falling off of their seats laughing or having tears in their eyes. For a while, I assumed that this was common for all teachers and was intrigued to hear some of the stories that other teachers had to tell.

In my quest for more teachers' stories, I decided to go to the Teacher's Educational Supplement (TES) website and asked a simple question in one of the forums. 'What stories do you have about teaching that really stick out to you?' I'll be honest, I did not expect the responses that I got which were both utterly disappointing and truly eye-opening at the same time.

I got a few responses but the stories that I got were unbelievably tame, if they were scenes in a movie it would be rated PG or maybe twelve at a push. While awaiting more responses the idea popped into my head that when I do get a bunch of good stories, as they were surely about to come flooding in at any moment, I could put them together and make a book filled with teachers' most interesting tales. I then posted another comment on the thread informing people of my amazing idea and it was at this point that I remembered why I hated school as a teenager; because some teachers are complete cunts and ruin everything fun for everyone.

A few people responded with nice little comments, wishing me well on my endeavour whether they were willing to contribute or not but the amount of condescending, snarky comments I got was unreal. 'Oh, would you like US to type the WHOLE BOOK for you?' Someone wrote. Another went with, 'how dare you ask other people to do your work so that you can get the credit!' Then there was the fuck face who wrote, 'it was very sneaky of you to not tell us that you were putting it in a book, I DO NOT give permission for you to use my story!' Sneaky? I thought, really? This was an idea that I had literally just come up with and I immediately disclosed it without needing to, hardly the work of Dick Dastardly. Not only that but this person's story was so shit it wouldn't have made the cut anyway, although ironically it will now just so that you can see what their amazing revelation was, so here it goes.

'I became a teacher in September 2001 and in my first week 9/11 happened and loads of people died.'

That was it...That was their epic story that I was not allowed to steal. Now I'm not saying 9/11 was no big deal, obviously, it was catastrophic devastation but let's keep it real, this person lives in Manchester, England, it's been near enough two decades since it happened, they knew none of the victims as far as I can gather from this very, very brief message and everybody already knows that people died on 9/11. To top it off, after I wrote in the forum, 'if you don't want to contribute you don't have to, I just thought it was a good idea,' Captain Fuck Face then wrote, 'why on earth would anybody want a book about teachers' tragedies anyway? It's DISGUSTING and if anybody reads it they are DISGUSTING.' So if you're reading this, just know that there is a teacher in Manchester who thinks you're disgusting and you ought to be ashamed of yourself.

If you enjoyed reading this book please leave a comment on Amazon, it will appease Bezos The Overlord's algorithm and mean that the book gets recommended to more people. Finally, if you would like to keep up to date with any other content that I produce in the future, follow me on twitter @Marvin_Foe

Class dismissed.

ACKNOWLEDGEMENTS

I would like to give a massive thank you to my amazing partner and daughter who have put up with the constant tapping, from my phone initially and then even more annoyingly from the laptop keyboard, for many nights on end whilst I wrote this book. You have always supported me in everything that I have done and continue to do so until this very day. I love and appreciate you very much.

I would like to thank all of the friends, family, colleagues and students who have contributed to this book, no matter how large or small the contribution, whether you knew you were contributing or not.